INVERAWE
seasons cookbook

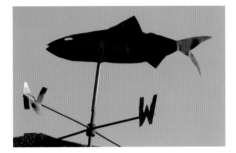

INVERAWE
seasons cookbook

Rosie Campbell-Preston

Quiller

First published in the UK in 2011
by Quiller, an imprint of Quiller Publishing Ltd

British Library Cataloguing-in-Publication Data
A catalogue record for this book is available
from the British Library

ISBN 978 1 84689 098 7

Designed and typeset by Paul Saunders
Printed in China

Quiller

An imprint of Quiller Publishing Ltd

Wykey House, Wykey, Shrewsbury, SY4 1JA
Tel: 01939 261616 Fax: 01939 261606
E-mail: info@quillerbooks.com
Website: www.countrybooksdirect.com

to Mum

contents

Acknowledgements

I would like to thank Maxine Clark for all her help with the recipes and her inspirational food styling. A big thank you, too, to Alan Donaldson for his food photography, and to John Gore, Lucy Burke and Joe Maclay for their photographs. I have also much appreciated the hard work, patience and attention to detail of my editor, Kirsty Ennever. Last but not least, heartfelt thanks to Robert, for once again being the most discerning recipe taster.

introduction

Inverawe seasons cookbook is another exciting collection of my favourite recipes. I have always enjoyed the contrasts of the four different seasons and the merry-go-round of flavours they inspire. I have tried to create dishes which reflect how I feel about food, as the colours change outside the window and the light eating of the warmer months gives way to a natural craving for heartier, more nourishing foods.

I adore the spring. It's the early wakening call when everything comes out of hibernation and bursts into life. Flavours are fresh, new and light after the solid, rich foods of the colder months. The Smoked Trout and Trout Caviar Mousse, smooth but peppered with the wonderful popping sensation of the trout eggs, is just made for Easter.

Summer evokes family picnics, alfresco dining, excursions and holidays for me. Paella, salads, roulades and pies are delicious and handy for outside eating.

By the time autumn arrives, it is a chance to move indoors again and catch up with friends. A time for simple entertaining, with quick easy dishes, like Smoked Sea Bass Korma with almonds and cashews or Smoked Venison and Red Wine Risotto.

Winter arrives bringing the first flurries of snow, cold frosty mornings and open log fires. The soup pot is back on the Aga and I need warm, sustaining, easy food such as Roast Smoked Salmon Cobbler or Celeriac and Smoked Haddock Gratin.

These recipes are simple, honest and easy to make. Just start with the best of ingredients, treat them with respect and you can't fail. My only tip, which I was told a long time ago, is to read through the recipe at least twice before you start – it's amazing what you can miss the first time! I hope you enjoy this second collection of recipes and that you have fun trying something new.

Happy cooking and enjoy!

Rosie Campbell Preston

Inverawe Smokehouses, a family business

The great adventure started all those years ago when I married Robert and found myself heading north to Argyll to be the wife of a fish farmer! It was quite a culture shock compared to my sheltered life in Windsor, but I instantly loved the wild remoteness of Scotland's West Coast.

We started the smokehouse as the result of a catastrophe. At the end of 1977 there was a terrible gale and we could only stand and watch as the waves destroyed our fish farm. It happened during Christmas week, so by the New Year it was plain that we had to think of something else. That was when Robert decided to have a business on land and with his past experience decided to start a smokery. From then on it took sheer determination and hard work to rebuild the fish farm and start the smokery. I still remember the excitement when Robert appeared in the kitchen with the first side of smoked Loch Etive trout – it was fantastic.

Little did I know that this was to be the beginning of my own business life. Until then, I had been bringing up our four lovely children, running the house and helping on the fish farm – gutting the odd ton of fish! With Robert proving to be a complete natural at smoking fish, I found myself in charge of the mail-order business. It was fun right from the start and I loved creating new and exciting recipes and serving suggestions for the catalogues.

It has been an amazing journey for us. We have worked hard, learned an awful lot and had plenty of fun. With the next generation now preparing to take a leading role – and as long as people want properly smoked fish – Inverawe is here to stay.

smoking the Inverawe way

Smoking is a truly artisan way of preserving foods. It is a natural process, using sustainable raw materials. There are faster, mass production methods but at Inverawe we have held on to the more skilful, natural way of smoking fish. The most important ingredient in the smoking process is time. Time for the fish to take up the salt; time for the fish to take up the smoke in the smokeboxes; time for the fish to cool before being packed. It is this time-giving process that naturally preserves the fish.

There are two methods of smoking: cold-smoking produces your traditional smoked salmon while hot-smoking cooks the fish to produce a delicate flavour but a more meaty texture.

In cold smoking the fish is gently smoked over oak-log fires. The continual drift of warm, sweet-smelling smoke, allows the fish to take up the natural preservatives and flavours of the oak smoke in its own unhurried time. The temperature never goes above 28°C (82°F) so this can take up to two or three days, depending on the size of the fish. The salmon is ready when the oil is just beginning to rise to the surface and the skin is easy to peel from the flesh.

SMOKING THE INVERAWE WAY

Hot smoking is the complete opposite. The fish is smoked over a low heat which gradually increases, until the fire-box lid is removed, to finally hot-smoke and cook the fish. This produces a fully cooked and smoked product. It is worth noting that 'hot smoke', 'roast smoke' and 'flaky' are all the same products.

Before going into the smoke the fish is cured or salted. This is as much for taste as it is for naturally preserving the fish. The salt intensifies the flavour of the fish by drawing out the excess water. This process firms up the flesh and concentrates all the good natural oils. Curing times vary with different fish and their oil content.

Being real traditionalists, we still use brick kilns and oak-log fires. We try to emulate the process of the original smoking kilns as closely as we can. We are totally dependent on the weather. The perfect smoking weather is a good south-westerly wind, the worst a cold, damp, still day, which is very rare in this part of the world. Each kiln has its own Inverawe 'fire box'. This is our own design – an oak-log fire on wheels. It is very simple, controlled manually by an adjustable flap at the base, and once the fire is going with a good heart, it will smoulder gently for hours. At peak times the fires are kept going 24/7, being stoked by hand every five hours.

The result of smoking 'the Inverawe way' is a full-bodied, robust and smoky flavour, instantly recognisable and unique to Inverawe.

spring recipes

smoked salmon koulibiaca

This is one of the best party dishes ever – it is perfect for large numbers and can be made well in advance. Once assembled and cooled, just cover with clingfilm and leave in the fridge until needed, then pop it into the oven just before you serve the first course. Serve it cut in slices, with a large bowl of mixed-leaf salad tossed in a sharp lemony dressing.

SERVES 4–6

75 g (3 oz) butter
6 spring onions, chopped
125 g (4 oz) button mushrooms, roughly chopped
75 g (3 oz) long grain rice
225 ml (8 fl oz) light fish stock
400 g (14 oz) roast smoked salmon
2 large eggs, hard-boiled, roughly chopped
1–2 tablespoons chopped fresh dill
3 tablespoons chopped fresh parsley
grated zest and juice of ½ lemon
1 x 375 g (14 oz) pack of ready-rolled puff pastry
25 g (1 oz) melted butter, to butter baking tray
1 egg, lightly beaten
salt and freshly ground black pepper

> **TIP**
> For a special occasion, shape into a fish.

1. Preheat the oven to Fan 200°C/220°C/425°F/Gas Mark 7. Melt the butter in a medium saucepan and add the spring onions and mushrooms and cook for 2–3 minutes. Stir in the rice, mix well then pour in the fish stock. Bring up to the boil, turn down the heat to low, cover and simmer for 12 minutes. Remove from the heat, uncover and set aside until completely cold.

2. Break the roast smoked salmon into large flakes and place in a bowl. Roughly chop the hard-boiled eggs and add to the salmon with half the chopped dill and half the parsley, mixing well. Taste and season. Tip the rice into another bowl and use a fork to fluff it up, then mix in the remaining dill and parsley and the lemon zest and juice, taste and season.

3. Unroll the pastry onto a lightly floured work surface and re-roll to make a larger rectangle. Spoon half the rice mix along the centre of the pastry, widthways, leaving a good bit of pastry at either side that will eventually wrap over the filling. Leave a border of at least 2.5 cm (1 inch) at either end.

4. Carefully spoon the salmon mix evenly over the rice, piling it high. You may want to use your hands to mould this into shape. Top with the remaining rice mix, pressing and moulding into a loaf shape.

5. Bring one side of the pastry up and over the filling, brush the edge with beaten egg, then bring the other side over to enclose the filling completely. Pinch the ends to seal. Carefully flip the parcel over so that the sealed edges are underneath on the base. Lift onto a buttered baking tray. Brush the surface of the pastry all over with beaten egg. If you like, use extra pastry to cut into fish shapes to decorate the pastry, then glaze again.

6. Bake for 20–25 minutes until deep golden brown. Remove from the oven and leave to rest for about 10 minutes before slicing to serve.

oriental smoked halibut soup

This will certainly put the zing into spring! I love to make this soup for lunch – it is packed with crunchy goodness. Make this as hot or as mild as you like with more or less chilli.

3 tablespoons sunflower oil
1 large leek, finely sliced
1 large carrot, julienned or grated
45 g (1½ oz) fresh ginger, julienned
3 garlic cloves, peeled and finely
    sliced
1 red and 1 green chilli, finely sliced
    (seeded if you don't like it too hot!)
a pinch of ground cumin
600 ml (1 pint) vegetable or fish
    stock
juice and zest of 1–2 limes
1 x 375 g (12 oz) pack fresh stir-fry
    rice noodles
a handful of coriander sprigs
sesame oil (optional)
200 g (7 oz) smoked halibut,
    shredded
toasted sesame seeds, to serve

1. Gently sauté the leek, carrot, ginger, garlic, and chillies in the oil. Stir in cumin, add stock, lime juice and zest and simmer for about 5–6 minutes until softened but still al dente.

2. Stir the noodles and coriander sprigs into the soup just before serving, and sprinkle with a couple of drops of sesame oil if liked.

3. Serve piping hot, with the shredded smoked halibut added at the last minute, and sprinkled with the toasted sesame seeds.

17

smoked mackerel and watercress pâté

This makes a gorgeous sandwich filling (on brown bread with extra watercress) for packing into a haversack or picnic hamper, but will just as easily serve as a quick pâté starter with some crunchy melba toast for a dinner party. It can even be piled onto crostini for a nibble with drinks. This recipe is equally good made with roast smoked salmon.

SERVES 4

150 g (5 oz) fresh watercress
200 g (7 oz) smoked mackerel fillet
100 g (3½ oz) Philadelphia cream
    cheese
4 tablespoons plain yoghurt
2 teaspoons creamed horseradish or
    a squeeze of Japanese wasabi
    paste, to taste (strong!)
grated zest and juice of 1 small
    lemon or 1 large lime
salt and freshly ground black pepper

1. Rinse the watercress well under cold water, remove any tough stalks then pat dry with kitchen paper.

2. Remove any skin from the mackerel, check and remove any stray bones then break into pieces and place in a food processor. Add the watercress, cream cheese, yoghurt and horseradish or wasabi and lemon or lime zest, process until roughly blended, then scrape out into a bowl and beat in enough lemon or lime juice to taste. Taste again and season with salt and pepper if you think it needs it.

3. Cover and chill for 1–2 hours before serving, to allow the flavours to develop.

4. Use generously in brown bread sandwiches, cramming in extra watercress on top, or dollop onto individual plates with extra watercress as a salad alongside a generous pile of melba toast.

> TIP
> This is particularly good if you replace the lemon or lime zest and juice with a couple of pieces of finely chopped Indian lime pickle.

18

smoked trout and trout caviar mousse

Brilliant as a starter or a light lunch. The sensation of the trout eggs exploding on your tongue is a refreshing surprise and has to be experienced to be believed.

SERVES 6

sunflower oil for greasing
4 tablespoons chopped fresh dill
100 ml (4 fl oz) good fish or
  vegetable stock
2 teaspoons powdered gelatine
200 g (7 oz) sliced cold-smoked
  trout or salmon, roughly chopped
about 2 tablespoons fresh lemon
  juice, to taste
175 ml (6 fl oz) double cream, chilled
100 g (2 pots) trout caviar, plus extra
  to serve
salt, if necessary

1. Line a straight-sided 500 ml (16 fl oz) mould or soufflé dish or six individual moulds or dishes with clingfilm, press down into the base and sides to smooth then lightly oil. Sprinkle with the chopped dill to coat like breadcrumbs.

2. Put the fish stock into a small saucepan and sprinkle on the gelatine. Leave to sponge and swell for 1 minute. Gently heat over a low heat until the gelatine is dissolved (do not let it boil or it may not set later) and then cool to room temperature.

3. Put the chopped trout, lemon juice and cooled gelatine mix into a food processor and blend until smooth.

4. With the machine running, pour in the cream and blend quickly until smooth. Do not overwork the mixture or it will curdle and go grainy. Taste and check for salt – it may not need any. Scoop out into a bowl and gently fold in the trout caviar. Spoon into the mould/s and smooth the top/s. Cover and chill for at least 12 hours or up to 2 days.

5. To unmould mousse, turn out and carefully peel off the clingfilm.

6. Serve with extra trout caviar and salad leaves.

21

mackerel and leek fritters with rhubarb sauce

I make this in spring when the first rhubarb appears. The sauce is a scaled-down version of a favourite chutney and it has just the right balance of tartness and acidity to cut through the rich smoked mackerel; it is my version of the classic combination of mackerel and gooseberry. You can of course use gooseberries if you are making the recipe in the late summer. It is equally delicious made with whatever is in the garden!

SERVES 4

FOR THE SAUCE
450 g (1 lb) rhubarb, trimmed & diced
   or 450 g (1 lb) gooseberries
1 small apple, peeled and diced
1 small red onion, finely chopped
1 tablespoon grated fresh ginger
2 tablespoons sweet chilli sauce
1 tablespoon red wine vinegar
about 2 teaspoons sugar, or to taste

FOR THE FRITTERS
350 g (12 oz) leeks, trimmed weight
1 onion, finely chopped
150 ml (¼ pint) light olive oil
225 g (8 oz) smoked mackerel fillets,
   skinned and flaked
1 fresh red chilli, seeded and sliced
   (optional)
3 tablespoons chopped fresh parsley
55 g (2 oz) self-raising flour
1 teaspoon baking powder
¼ teaspoon ground turmeric
   (optional)
1 large egg
75 ml (2½ fl oz) milk
1 teaspoon cumin seeds
salt and freshly ground black pepper

For the sauce

Put everything together in a saucepan with 75 ml (2½ fl oz) water. Bring to the boil, stirring occasionally. Reduce heat to medium-low, cover and simmer for 15 to 20 minutes or until the rhubarb is tender. Uncover and simmer, stirring occasionally, until thickened, about 5 minutes more. Set aside and serve warm or cold. If it is too thick, just let it down with a little extra water.

For the fritters

1. Thickly slice the leeks, rinse and drain well. Heat half the olive oil in a large frying pan and sauté the leeks with the onion over a medium heat for about 15 minutes, or until soft. Transfer to a large bowl and add the flaked smoked mackerel, chilli, parsley, and season with black pepper. Allow to cool.

2. In another bowl sift the flour, baking powder and turmeric together, then whisk in the egg and milk to form a batter. Add the cumin seeds. Gently fold this batter into the leek and mackerel mixture.

3. Heat a couple of tablespoons of the remaining olive oil in a large frying pan and fry large spoonfuls of the mixture over a medium heat for 2–3 minutes on each side, or until golden and crisp. Remove and drain on kitchen paper. Keep warm while you fry the remainder in the remaining olive oil.

4. Serve warm, with the sauce on the side or drizzled over.

roast smoked salmon and courgette filo pie

This will fill you full of the joys of spring! It's a tart not unlike the Greek spinach and feta *spanakopita*, moist and packed full of goodness. A favourite for a light lunch, part of a cold buffet or even carried to a picnic still in the tin. A tomato and onion salad is just perfect with it.

SERVES 6–8

5 large eggs
350 g (12 oz) courgettes, very thinly sliced into rounds
125 g (4 oz) bulgur wheat
100 ml (4 fl oz) decent olive oil, plus extra for brushing
125 g (4 oz) freshly grated Parmesan cheese
finely grated zest of 1 lemon
fresh lemon juice, to taste
225 g (8–9 oz) packet Greek-style filo pastry
200 g (7 oz) roast smoked salmon, flaked
3 tablespoons chopped fresh basil
salt and freshly ground black pepper

1. Beat the eggs in a large bowl and stir in the courgettes to coat them completely. Mix in the bulgur wheat, the olive oil, lemon zest and Parmesan and season with a little salt and lots of pepper. Taste and add a dash of lemon juice – remember the salmon may be salty, so don't add too much salt at this stage. Cover and leave to stand for an hour.

2. Preheat the oven to Fan 160°C/180°C/350°F/Gas Mark 4 and set a baking sheet inside.

3. Brush a 20.5 cm (8 inch) springform tin with olive oil. Carefully unroll the filo pastry – watch out as it can tear! Cut the stack in two through all thicknesses and re-stack. Remove one sheet at a time, keeping the rest under a damp tea towel so it doesn't dry out. Lay one sheet into the tin, lightly pressing it down into the base and up the side. Don't worry if it tears now – it won't be seen in the finished dish. Gently brush this layer with a little olive oil. Lay the next sheet just overlapping the first, and covering a further bit of the tin, and brush with oil. Repeat with the remaining filo until the base and sides are covered.

4. Gently stir the flaked salmon and basil into the courgette mixture and then ladle it into the filo pastry case, spreading it out evenly. Trim any straggly bits of filo hanging over the sides of the tin.

5. Bake for 45–50 minutes on the hot baking sheet. Remove from the oven and cool until just warm before removing it from the tin to serve. Very good with a tomato salad and delicious eaten cold.

smoked salmon ravioli with creamy dill sauce

A dish to impress and good fun to make if you have a bit of time to spare – the ravioli can be frozen until you are ready to cook and serve them. I have used a creamy dill sauce, but you can make a lighter sauce, and serve the ravioli bathed in a light fish or chicken broth – very Italian!

SERVES 8
(MAKES ABOUT 36–42)

FOR THE PASTA
400 g (14 oz) Italian 00 flour (or plain white flour)
2 medium eggs, beaten
3 egg yolks

FOR THE SMOKED SALMON FILLING
400 g (14 oz) smoked salmon
2 medium eggs
200 ml (7 fl oz) double cream
2 teaspoons chopped fresh chives or chervil

FOR THE CREAMY DILL SAUCE
55 g (2 oz) butter
4 spring onions, chopped
4 tablespoons dry white wine or vermouth
250 ml (8 fl oz) double cream
2 tablespoons chopped fresh dill
fresh lemon juice
salt and freshly ground black pepper
toasted pine nuts, capers and a few currants, to serve

1. Place the flour in a mound on a clean work surface. Use your fist to make a large well in the centre – a ring of flour to contain the eggs. Pour the 2 beaten eggs and 3 egg yolks into the well. Slowly pull and flick the flour into the eggs, mixing with your fingers until it is all incorporated. Once it has formed a rough ball, knead it briskly by hand (for about 5 minutes), until smooth and shiny. If it feels very soft at this stage, work in some more flour. If too dry, just add a tablespoon of water, but the dough should be firm, firmer than bread dough. Put into a plastic bag and leave to rest at room temperature for 30 minutes. When rested, the dough will be softer and easier to roll out.

2. Now make the filling. Put the smoked salmon and eggs into a food processor and blend until smooth. With the machine running, slowly add the cream until the mixture thickens, then add the chopped chives or chervil, and freshly ground black pepper to taste. Mix well.

3. Divide the pasta in half and roll out each half through a pasta roller as thin as you can – about setting number 6, depending on your machine. Do this by setting the rollers to the widest setting and winding your dough through. Adjust to the next setting and roll the dough through again, carrying on in this manner until you have stretched it out to about setting 6.

4. Cut the pasta into manageable sheets, place on trays lined with lightly floured tea towels and cover with clingfilm to prevent it drying out.

5. To assemble, dust a clean work surface with a little extra flour (semolina flour is useful here – being a coarser flour, it will fall off the ravioli when you cook it. Finer flours tend to stick and cook to a 'jelly' on the outside of the pasta). Lay out half the pasta sheets. Divide the smoked salmon filling into approximately 42 equal-sized portions (large teaspoonfuls really!) and place each one 5 cm (2 inches) apart on the pasta sheets.

6. Brush the pasta between the mounds of salmon with a little cold water. Cover with

26

the remaining sheets of pasta, carefully making sure all the air is excluded around each mound as you press them closed. Cut the ravioli out using a pastry wheel or biscuit cutter. Cover and refrigerate or open-freeze, then pack into boxes between layers of freezer film, until you are ready to use.

7. To make the sauce, fry the spring onions in the butter for 5 minutes, splash in the wine and reduce until almost dry. Pour in the cream, add the dill and simmer until slightly thickened. Season to taste with a little lemon juice, salt and pepper. Set aside.

8. When ready to serve, bring a large pot of salted water to the boil, add the ravioli, and cook for about 3 minutes. Take 2–3 tablespoons of the cooking water and add to the sauce. (This helps season and stabilise the sauce as the cooking water contains starch and salt.) Drain the ravioli well through a colander, return to the pan and add the sauce. Gently mix and warm through.

9. Serve in warm bowls topped with toasted pine nuts, a few capers and currants.

guacamole with smoked salmon and poppadoms

I love this combination of fresh, sharp guacamole with rich, creamy smoked salmon. For an even smoother taste add a spoonful of crème fraîche to the guacamole.

2 ripe avocados, halved, stoned and peeled
juice of 1–2 limes (depending on juiciness!)
½ onion, grated
1 green chilli, seeded and very finely chopped
2 tablespoons chopped fresh coriander
salt and freshly ground black pepper
200 g (7 oz) sliced smoked salmon, to serve
mini poppadoms, to serve

1. To make the guacamole, put the avocado into a bowl with the lime juice, roughly mash up with a fork, then mix in the onion, chilli and coriander. Season to taste with salt and pepper and extra lime juice. Cover and set aside.

2. Serve spoonfuls on plates with a pile of smoked salmon and spicy poppadoms.

29

smoked eel caesar salad

Why has no one done this before – it makes a fantastic spring lunch, and is full of robust flavours and texture. Eel and anchovy go so well together – the anchovy brings out the smoky sweetness of the eel. It's a good picnic salad too as it stands up to being packed in a plastic box, only to be dressed on site.

SERVES 4

400 g (14 oz) smoked eel

FOR THE CROUTONS
200 g (7 oz) white bread, cut into
   small cubes
75 ml (3 fl oz) olive oil

FOR THE CAESAR DRESSING
150 g (5 oz) Parmesan, grated
2 tablespoons white wine vinegar
250 g (9 oz) ready-made mayonnaise
3 tablespoons Dijon mustard
1 teaspoon creamed horseradish
2 anchovy fillets, rinsed
1 garlic clove, crushed
3 tablespoons olive oil
1 Cos or Romaine lettuce, trimmed
   and torn into pieces
salt and freshly ground black pepper

TO SERVE
12 anchovy fillets, drained
55 g (2 oz) Parmesan shavings

1. Preheat the oven to Fan 180°C/200°C/400°F/Gas Mark 6.

2. For the croutons, scatter the cubed bread onto a baking tray, sprinkle with salt and drizzle with the oil. Bake for 5–6 minutes, or until the croutons are golden-brown, giving them an occasional stir. Remove from the oven and set aside.

3. For the Caesar dressing, place the grated Parmesan and vinegar into a food processor (or use a hand blender) and blend until very smooth. Add the mayonnaise, mustard, horseradish, anchovy fillets, garlic and olive oil and blend again until smooth and creamy. Season to taste (and let down with a little milk if too thick).

4. Place the lettuce into a large bowl, pour on some dressing and gently turn the leaves to coat them. Mix in half the croutons and pile the salad into four separate shallow bowls. Add three whole anchovy fillets to each bowl and drizzle over a little more dressing.

5. Tear or cut the eel into large pieces and arrange over each bowl of salad. Sprinkle with Parmesan shavings and remaining croutons and serve.

> **TIP**
> Brush the eel with Japanese soy sauce or teriyaki marinade and place under the grill for a couple of minutes to warm through, then use to top the salad.

spring dips

creamy smoked salmon, potato and wild garlic dip

SERVES 4–6

450 g (1 lb) floury potatoes, peeled
30 g (generous 1 oz) fresh wild garlic
    leaves or substitute with chives or
    spring onions
200 g (7 oz) smoked salmon,
    chopped (any smoked fish
    works well)
juice of ½ lemon, or more
1 teaspoon cider vinegar
150 ml (5 fl oz) light olive oil
salt and freshly ground black pepper
warm pitta bread, to serve

In spring, we find masses of wild garlic up here at Inverawe – a sure sign that summer is on its way! It loses its flavour somewhat when cooked, but used as a herb, like chives or spring onions, it is fantastic. Serve the dip with warm pitta bread.

Boil the potatoes, and while they are boiling, wash the wild garlic leaves very well, pat dry and chop finely. Drain the potatoes and mash until very smooth. Cool slightly. Stir in half the smoked salmon, all the wild garlic, lemon juice and vinegar. Now slowly add the olive oil into the mix, tablespoon by tablespoon, beating with an electric hand mixer, as if you were making mayonnaise. Continue until the oil is all used up and the mix is fairly smooth (do not be tempted to use a food processor as this will make the potato mix go very gloopy). Stir in the remaining smoked salmon. Season with salt, pepper and lemon juice to taste, and serve immediately while still warm.

> **TIP**
> I sometimes replace a couple of tablespoons of the olive oil with walnut or hazelnut oil if I have it. Delicious!

'some like it hot' smoked salmon dip

SERVES 8

349 g pack firm silken tofu, drained
2 chopped Roquito™ peppers,
    drained (Merchant Gourmet)
1–2 teaspoons Cajun spice blend
    (salt, black pepper, cayenne
    pepper, onion powder, chilli
    powder, garlic powder, thyme,
    basil and bay leaf), to taste
2–3 tablespoons fresh lemon juice,
    to taste
400 g (14 oz) roast smoked salmon
3 spring onions, finely chopped
1 tablespoon chopped fresh dill

Tofu is a great substitute for cream cheese in a dish – and so much healthier, and good for those with dairy intolerances. Make this as hot and spicy as you like by adding more chopped peppers and Cajun spice.

1. Put the tofu, chopped peppers, Cajun spice blend and lemon juice into a food processor or blender and blend until smooth.

2. Add the salmon and spring onions and blend again until smooth. Stir in the dill, taste and season.

3. Cover and chill until ready to serve with tortilla chips.

Inverawe sushi

I was never a great fan of sushi until I was shown how to make it by a charming Japanese lady who came to visit us at the Smokehouse. We had great fun in the kitchen, and I realised that once the rice is cooked properly and a little care is taken with the moulding, it's not too difficult. That said, the recipe will never meet the exacting standards of a real sushi chef, but it tastes wonderful, and looks pretty good too!

MAKES ABOUT 20 PIECES

FOR THE VINEGARED RICE
400 ml Japanese rice (measure by volume, not weight for this)
7 tablespoons Japanese rice vinegar
2½ tablespoons caster sugar
2 teaspoons sea salt

FOR THE TOPPINGS
4 medium-sized raw, shell-on tiger prawns (no heads)
200 g (7 oz) royal fillet or par-smoked trout fillet, skinned
200 g (7 oz) sliced smoked sea bass
200 g (7 oz) smoked mackerel fillet, trimmed
2 teaspoons wasabi paste or powder
shiso micro greens, Japanese soy sauce and pickled ginger, to serve

1. Put the rice in a large sieve and wash under cold running water until the water runs clear. Soak the rice in cold water for 10–15 minutes and then drain well. Transfer to a heavy-based saucepan, pour in 460 ml water, cover and bring to the boil. Once boiling, lower the heat and simmer, covered, for about 10 minutes or until all the water has been absorbed. Without removing the lid take off the heat and leave to stand for about 10–15 minutes.

2. Mix 3 tablespoons of the rice vinegar, sugar and salt in a small jug or bowl and stir until dissolved. Spoon the cooked rice into a large, shallow baking dish. Sprinkle generously with the vinegar dressing. Use a wooden spatula to fold the vinegar dressing into the rice. Do not stir, but gently fold. Let the rice cool to room temperature before using to make the sushi.

3. Mix together the remaining rice vinegar with 250 ml (8 fl oz) cold water for the hand-dipping vinegar in a small bowl and set aside.

4. Skewer a cocktail stick through each prawn from top to tail to prevent curling while cooking. Blanch in boiling water for 2 minutes until lightly cooked and pink. Drain and put under cold running water. Remove and discard the cocktail sticks, peel off the shell and remove back vein from each prawn. Make a slit up the belly lengthways and open out (butterfly). Slice the royal fillet or par-smoked trout fillet, sea bass and mackerel fillet into rectangular pieces about 7 cm x 3 cm.

5. If using wasabi powder, mix with 2 teaspoons water in an egg cup and stir well to make a clay-like consistency. Leave upside down to prevent drying.

6. Wet your hands in the hand-vinegar and take about 1–2 tablespoons of the cooked rice and mould into rectangular cylinders – about 5 cm x 2 cm x 2 cm. Put a small dot of wasabi on top of each rice cylinder and cover with the fish or prawns. Cover and chill, but serve at room temperature.

7. Arrange on a platter and serve with pickled ginger and Japanese soy sauce in small dishes for dipping. Alternatively, serve as party canapés or on small plates as a starter.

TIP
This recipe can also be made into a delightful rice salad – carefully mix the vinegared rice with the diced fish, diced cucumber, and some chopped spring onions.

smoked salmon nasi goreng

I remember this dish being very popular in the late sixties and seventies and now it's back! It makes an interesting alternative to kedgeree. The Asian flavours bring out the best in the smoked salmon, but you can make this with any smoked fish – it will still be good. Dried shrimp paste can be substituted with Thai fish sauce, just double the amount, and ketjap manis is available from larger supermarkets and is a useful store cupboard stand-by.

SERVES 4

400 g (14 oz) roast smoked salmon
  or smoked mackerel fillets
2 tablespoons sunflower oil
250 g (9 oz) white long grain rice,
  cooked
8 spring onions, sliced or chopped
4 large eggs
2 x 57 g pots Morecambe Bay potted
  shrimps (or equivalent)
10 cm (4 inch) piece of cucumber,
  cut into chunks
4 tablespoons soy sauce, for
  drizzling

FOR THE NASI GORENG PASTE
4–6 garlic cloves, roughly chopped
4 medium shallots, roughly chopped
55 g (2 oz) salted peanuts
1–2 fat green chillies, halved and
  seeded
1 tablespoon dried shrimp paste
4 tablespoons ketjap manis (sweet
  soy sauce)
2 tablespoons soy sauce

1. Roughly chop or flake the fish and set aside.

2. Now make the nasi goreng paste: put all the paste ingredients into a food processor and blend until as smooth as possible. Alternatively do this in a pestle and mortar if feeling strong!

3. Pour the sunflower oil into a hot wok and, working quickly, add 4 tablespoons of the paste, stir-fry for 30 seconds then tip in the cooked rice and boldly toss to coat with the sauce. Next add half the shrimps and their butter, the spring onions, then the chopped or flaked fish. Stir well and continue to cook for a couple of minutes until heated through. Pull off the heat but keep warm.

4. Fry one egg per person, keeping the yolks runny.

5. Add the cucumber to the rice just before serving. Serve immediately in warm bowls, each serving topped with a fried egg and the remaining warmed shrimps, drizzled with soy sauce.

smoked duck and spring onion pancakes

Try these for Pancake Day/Shrove Tuesday – they are easy to make and very moreish! If short of time, then you can buy ready-made Chinese pancakes or even small wheat flour tortillas but homemade are always best, and children love them. My grandchildren wolf these down as fast as I can make them.

SERVES 4 (MAKES ABOUT 8 PANCAKES)

FOR THE SPRING ONION PANCAKES
125 g (4 oz) plain flour, sifted
pinch of salt
2 large eggs
200 ml (7 fl oz) milk
4 spring onions, finely chopped
55 g (2 oz) butter

FOR THE SMOKED DUCK FILLING
360 g (12 oz) sliced smoked duck
    breast
½ teaspoon Chinese five-spice
    powder
2 tablespoons light sesame oil
6 level tablespoons Chinese hoisin
    sauce
freshly ground black pepper

FOR THE VEGETABLES
1 bunch spring onions, very finely
    shredded
½ cucumber, halved, seeds removed
    and finely sliced diagonally
1 red pepper, halved, seeded and
    very thinly shredded

1. Put the flour into a food processor with a pinch of salt, the eggs and milk. Blend until smooth. (Alternatively you can do this with a hand blender.) It should look like thin cream. Pour into a jug and stir in the finely chopped spring onions.

2. Melt the butter in a small pan. Spoon a couple of tablespoons of it into the pancake batter and whisk it in. Keep the remaining melted butter in a small pot for greasing the pancake pan between pancakes. Cover the batter and leave to rest for 20 minutes.

3. Meanwhile, you can prepare the vegetables, placing each type in a separate bowl.

4. Once the batter has rested, heat a small non-stick frying pan to medium. Grease the pan with a little butter. Stir the batter then pour in enough batter to thinly cover the base of the pan. Quickly pour any excess liquid batter back into the jug. Cook for about half a minute, lifting the edge with a palette knife to see if it is browning. Turn over and cook on the other side for a few seconds only. Slide out of the pan onto a plate and cover with a square of greaseproof paper to stop the pancakes sticking together. Set the plate over a pan of simmering water, to keep warm whilst you make the rest. Cover the stack with foil.

5. Cut the smoked duck into thin strips and toss in the five-spice and pepper. Gently heat the sesame oil in a frying pan or wok and add the duck. Stir-fry for a couple of minutes until heated through, then add the hoisin sauce. Continue to stir-fry for about 1 minute, until the duck is glistening and coated in sauce.

6. Pile the duck onto a warmed dish, serve with the bowls of prepared vegetables and the pile of pancakes. Now give a demonstration of how to fill your pancake – top a pancake with some duck, spring onions, red pepper and cucumber, then roll up and eat! Invite everyone to dig in, and watch those pancakes disappear!

38

summer recipes

Inverawe smoky summer paella

Adding some Morecambe Bay shrimps to this recipe adds a touch of seaside luxury . . . just try it! Using the smoked mussel oil instead of olive oil will really intensify the smoky flavour. We also added some squid rings, but these are not to everyone's taste.

SERVES 6

4 tablespoons good olive oil
1 large onion, finely chopped
2 cloves garlic, finely chopped
2 large red peppers, chopped or
    sliced
450 g (1 lb) Spanish paella rice
150 ml (¼ pint) dry white wine
a good pinch of dried red chilli
    flakes
2 teaspoons sweet paprika
about 1.2 litres (2 pints) fish or
    vegetable stock
a large pinch of saffron strands,
    soaked in 3 tablespoons hot water
6 ripe tomatoes, quartered
250 g (9 oz) smoked mussels in oil,
    drained
12 whole raw prawns, in their shells
2 x 57 g pots Morecambe Bay
    shrimps
55 g (2 oz) raw squid rings (optional)
125 g (4 oz) fresh or frozen peas
400 g (14 oz) roast smoked salmon
4 tablespoons chopped flat leaf
    parsley
lemon or lime wedges, to serve
salt and freshly ground black pepper

1. Heat the olive oil (or the oil from the smoked mussels if preferred) in a paella pan or large deep frying pan. Add the onion, garlic and peppers and cook for about 5 minutes until softened, stirring occasionally. Stir in the rice until all the grains are nicely coated with oil and glossy.

2. Pour in the wine, bring to the boil and allow to bubble and reduce until it disappears. Stir in the chilli flakes, paprika, fish stock, and soaked saffron. Stir well, bring to the boil then turn down the heat and simmer gently for 10 minutes.

3. Now stir in the tomatoes, smoked mussels and prawns and squid (if using) and cook gently for 5 minutes before finally adding the shrimps and their butter, the peas and the roast smoked salmon, tucking this into the rice. Cook for another 5 minutes until heated through. Season to taste.

4. At this stage, almost all the liquid will have been absorbed and the rice will be tender. Scatter the chopped parsley over the top and serve immediately, straight from the pan, with a big pile of lemon or lime wedges on the side. This is messy food, so have plenty of paper napkins around.

smoked salmon with fennel, lemon and radish salad

I was lucky enough to have a glut of fennel in the garden and came up with this deliciously fresh and crunchy salad to serve with any smoked fish. The aniseed crunch of fennel, the spicy radish and the tart lemon make the ultimate salad.

SERVES 4

1 bulb of fresh fennel, trimmed
3 radishes
1 whole fresh lemon
2 tablespoons decent olive oil
2 spring onions, sliced
a good squeeze of lemon juice
salt and freshly ground black pepper
200 g (7 oz) smoked salmon, to
  serve

1. Using a thin sharp knife or a mandolin, slice the fennel and radishes as thinly as you can. Toss them with the olive oil, salt and pepper.

2. Peel the lemon with a sharp knife to remove all the skin and pith, like an apple.

3. Cut out the segments and add them to the fennel and radishes. Cover and leave to soften slightly for 10 minutes.

4. Taste and season with a dash of lemon juice, salt and pepper and sprinkle with the sliced spring onions.

5. To serve, divide the salmon between 4 plates and arrange salad alongside.

45

salmon niçoise

I fell in love with this salad when I was in France. It's a complete meal in itself but I like to serve it with lots of French bread and a Provençal rosé to evoke all those wonderful memories of family holidays in the sun.

SERVES 4–6

400 g (14 oz) roast smoked salmon, flaked

FOR THE DRESSING

6 tablespoons olive oil

2 tablespoons white wine vinegar or lemon juice

½ teaspoon Dijon mustard

2 tablespoons salted capers, rinsed and drained

3 tablespoons chopped fresh herbs (parsley, basil, chives and tarragon)

FOR THE NIÇOISE SALAD

350 g (12 oz) small waxy potatoes (Anya are good)

175 g (6 oz) fine green beans, topped and tailed

2 large ripe tomatoes, quartered

200 g (7 oz) smoked mussels, drained

55 g (2 oz) black olives (Greek-style are good for this)

3 hard-boiled eggs, peeled and quartered

1. Whisk all the dressing ingredients together and set aside.

2. Boil the potatoes in salted water for 15 minutes or until tender, adding the green beans about 4 minutes before the potatoes are ready. Drain them and thickly slice the potatoes. Put the potatoes and beans into a bowl and pour over a splash of dressing. Mix the potatoes and beans with the tomatoes, anchovies and olives and tip out onto a large serving platter, re-arranging as you go. Add the flaked salmon. Scatter the eggs on top.

3. Quickly heat up the remaining dressing in a small pan, and when boiling, pour over the salad.

4. Serve with loads of crusty French bread and chilled rosé!

courgette, herb and smoked salmon roulade

When Robert arrived in the kitchen one day bearing a second basket of garden courgettes something had to be done! This roulade is delicious and an all-rounder for summer entertaining. It will be the star of any alfresco lunch and travels really well for picnics. Everyone will love it.

SERVES 4-6

450 g (1 lb) courgettes
4 medium eggs, separated
finely grated zest of 1 lemon
3 tablespoons chopped fresh herbs
    (marjoram, mint, parsley)
3 tablespoons freshly grated
    Parmesan cheese
salt and freshly ground black pepper
250 g (9 oz) smoked salmon,
    chopped
200 ml (7 fl oz) crème fraîche
fresh lemon juice, to taste
cayenne pepper
extra crème fraîche or soured
    cream, to serve
extra herbs, to serve

1. Preheat the oven to 170°CFan/190°C/375°F/Gas Mark 5.

2. Grease and line a 20 x 30 cm (8 x 12 inch) Swiss roll tin with non-stick baking parchment.

3. Coarsely grate the courgettes. Toss with salt in a colander and leave for 30 minutes. Rinse and squeeze dry. Beat in the egg yolks, lemon zest, herbs and Parmesan and season with salt and pepper.

4. In a separate bowl, whisk the egg whites with a pinch of salt until stiff but not dry, then fold them into the courgette mixture using a large metal spoon. Pour into the prepared tin and quickly level the mixture, spreading it out into the corners. Bake for 10–12 minutes until set and light golden brown.

5. Pulse half the salmon in a food processor with a little lemon juice until you have a coarse purée. Add the crème fraîche and pulse a few times until almost smooth. Season to taste with salt, cayenne and lemon juice. Beat in the remaining chopped smoked salmon. Cover and store in the fridge until required.

6. When the roulade is cooked, invert onto a clean tea towel. Carefully peel away the baking parchment and loosely roll up from the short side like a Swiss roll. Cool.

7. When cold, carefully unroll the roulade and spread with the filling. Roll up again from the short side, using the tea towel to help you, then carefully transfer to a serving plate, seam-side down. Cover and chill until ready to serve.

8. Serve cut into thick slices with soured cream or crème fraîche.

49

smoked salmon, garlic and goat's cheese tart

This is a very rich tart – perfect for a summer lunch party or as a starter if you make it into individual tartlets. If you can find only small goat's cheese logs with the rind on, make the filling with all the other ingredients, pour into the pastry shell then slice the goat's cheese and arrange on top. This will look very pretty when cooked.

SERVE 4–6

FOR THE CHEESE PASTRY
125 g (4 oz) unsalted butter, chilled and diced
55 g (2 oz) grated Gruyère cheese
275 g (10 oz) plain white flour
1 egg yolk

FOR THE FILLING
4 whole unpeeled garlic cloves
200 ml (7 fl oz) soured cream
4 tablespoons plain Greek yoghurt
250 g (9 oz) fresh soft goat's cheese (the kind with no rind)
3 medium eggs, beaten
2 teaspoons finely chopped fresh rosemary, plus a few extra sprigs to garnish
2 teaspoons sweet chilli sauce or a couple of dashes Tabasco
200 g (7 oz) smoked salmon, chopped
1 tablespoon fresh lemon juice
25 g (1 oz) pine nuts
salt and freshly ground black pepper

1. To make the pastry, blend the butter and cheese with the flour and a pinch of salt in a food processor, add the egg yolk and 1 tablespoon water and pulse in a few short bursts until it comes together. Knead lightly on a floured work surface until smooth. Wrap in clingfilm and chill for at least 30 minutes.

2. Meanwhile, put the garlic (unpeeled) into a small pan of boiling water and simmer for about 15 minutes until completely soft. Drain, cool and peel.

3. Use the pastry to line a 25 cm (9 inch) loose-based tart tin; trim off excess pastry. Prick the pastry all over the base and chill.

4. Preheat the oven to Fan 180° C/200°C/400°F/Gas Mark 6.

5. Put the soured cream, yoghurt, goat's cheese, beaten eggs, sweet chilli sauce or a drop or two of Tabasco, the chopped rosemary and peeled garlic cloves, in a food processor and blend until smooth. Now add the smoked salmon and pulse until almost blended, but still showing pink bits. Season to taste with lemon juice.

6. Pour the filling into the prepared pastry shell and scatter with pine nuts and rosemary sprigs.

7. Bake for about 30–45 minutes until puffed and golden brown, but still a bit wobbly. Remove from oven and allow to sit for at least 10 minutes before serving. Serve hot, warm or at room temperature, with a simple summer salad dressed with olive oil and lemon.

> TIP
> This tart is good re-heated and will freeze for up to 3 months.

chilled cucumber and fennel soup with smoked salmon

A heavenly chilled soup for a warm summer evening. It is a brilliant green colour, but I sometimes whisk in a good dollop of crème fraîche or soured cream for a special occasion, so that the colour changes to a pretty pastel green, which looks just as good and tastes divine.

SERVES 4

1 small Florence fennel bulb
2 spring onions, trimmed and chopped (include the green parts)
1 tablespoon extra virgin olive oil, plus extra to garnish
600 ml (1 pint) vegetable stock or potato water
a dash of gin (optional)
2 cucumbers, washed and coarsely grated (set 6 tablespoons aside for garnish)
100 g (3½ oz) sliced smoked salmon or royal fillet
fennel or dill sprigs, to garnish
salt and freshly ground black pepper

1. Trim the fronds off the fennel and reserve for garnish. Halve the fennel bulb and cut out the tough triangular core. Slice or chop the flesh finely. Heat the olive oil in a medium saucepan and add the fennel and spring onions and a splash of water to help it cook. Cover and simmer for 5 minutes until soft. Add the vegetable stock, bring to the boil and simmer for a further 5 minutes. Add the gin if using (only about 1 tablespoon), and stir in the cucumber (put the reserved cucumber into a small sieve or colander over a bowl until ready to serve – this will drain off excess water).

2. Transfer the soup to a liquidiser (not a food processor) and blend until smooth. (Alternatively do this in the pan with a hand blender.) Remove from the heat and strain through a coarse sieve into a metal bowl set in ice-cold water. Cooling the soup quickly will keep the colour nice and green. Taste and season, then chill.

3. To serve, cut the smoked salmon into strips or cube the fillet. Ladle the soup into wide, chilled, soup bowls, arranging the salmon and drained cucumber in a mound in the centre of each. Scatter the fennel or dill sprigs over and trickle a little olive oil around.

> **TIP**
> If you want to serve a bright green soup, but still want the luxury of the cream, spoon a blob into the centre of each bowl then top with the cucumber and smoked salmon. This soup is also particularly good drizzled with a few drops of lemon-infused olive oil.

baked tomatoes stuffed with rice and smoked sea bass, with a basil, caper and pine nut dressing

This dish is a real treat: dense white fish, ripe beef tomatoes bursting with the taste of sunshine and the fresh aroma of basil. It's just perfect for eating outdoors and can be served hot or cold. I love serving it at barbecues.

SERVES 4

4 large beef tomatoes

FOR THE STUFFING
2 tablespoons extra virgin olive oil
½ onion, finely chopped
2 garlic cloves, peeled and crushed
1 teaspoon smoked paprika
150 g (5 oz) Spanish paella rice or
  Italian risotto rice
about 200 ml (8 fl oz) light fish stock
3 tablespoons chopped fresh parsley
  or basil
1 tablespoon dry white vermouth
350 g (12 oz) smoked sea bass or
  similar, flaked

FOR THE BASIL, CAPER AND PINE NUT DRESSING
½ garlic clove
30 g (generous 1 oz) fresh basil
  leaves, no stalks
6 tablespoons extra virgin olive oil
2 tablespoons white wine vinegar
1 tablespoon salted capers, rinsed
  and chopped
3 tablespoons pine nuts
salt and freshly ground black pepper

1. Slice the tops off the tomatoes and scoop out the flesh inside. Turn the tomato shells upside down onto kitchen paper to drain and finely chop the tomato flesh and reserve.

2. Heat 2 tablespoons olive oil in a medium saucepan and add the onion and garlic. Stir to coat with the oil then cook for 5 minutes until beginning to soften but not brown. Add the paprika and rice and cook for 1 minute. Pour in the fish stock, bring to the boil, then cover and simmer over medium heat for about 15–20 minutes until the rice is cooked and has absorbed all the liquid but is still moist. (Give it a stir every now and then to prevent it sticking, but this is NOT risotto so don't over-stir or the rice will be claggy!) Add more stock or water if necessary if the rice dries out before it is cooked.

3. Preheat the oven to Fan 170°C/190°C/375°F/Gas Mark 5.

4. Now make the dressing. Put all the ingredients except the pine nuts and capers into a small blender and blend until smooth. Stir in the pine nuts and capers and season to taste.

5. Once the rice is cooked, stir in the reserved chopped tomato, the parsley and vermouth. Cook everything for another 2–3 minutes. Gently fold in the flaked sea bass. Taste and season with salt and pepper.

6. Fill each tomato with the fish and rice mixture and pop the lids back on. Bake the tomatoes for about 15 minutes and then serve hot, drizzled with the dressing. They are equally good cold.

smoked cod's roe mousse with herb and wine jelly

I make this for a pretty summer starter, as the whole thing can be made ahead. It is something that can be made in little individual pots (glass would be nice to show off the pink and green layers) or in one large dish from which to serve generous scoops. The herb and wine jelly not only looks delightful, tastes delicious but also seals the flavour into the mousse as it chills.

SERVES 6

FOR THE MOUSSE
225 g (8 oz) smoked cod's roe
2 anchovies in oil, drained and finely
    chopped
3 tablespoons light olive oil
juice of 1 lemon
15 g (½ oz) powdered gelatine
150 ml (¼ pint) double cream or
    crème fraîche
2 egg whites
1 tablespoon chopped chives or
    parsley (optional)

FOR THE HERB AND WINE JELLY
600 ml (1 pint) pale fish stock
150 ml (4 fl oz) dry white wine
3 tablespoons white wine vinegar
1 large shallot, finely diced
4 lightly crushed peppercorns
1 tablespoon powdered gelatine
1½ tablespoons chopped tarragon
2 tablespoons chopped parsley
1 tablespoon chopped dill or chervil
salt and freshly ground black pepper

1. Put the smoked cod's roe into a bowl, pour over enough boiling water to cover and leave to soak for 1 minute to loosen the skin. Drain, then peel off the skin. Return to the bowl then mash the roe with the anchovies and olive oil. Leave to stand for 15 minutes to soften, then beat with an electric hand mixer. Beat in the lemon juice until creamy and season with pepper. Fold in the herbs (if using).

2. Put 4 tablespoons of cold water into a saucepan, sprinkle in the gelatine and leave to soak for 5 minutes, then stir over low heat until the gelatine has dissolved (do not boil). Remove from the heat then stir in 2 extra tablespoons warm water. Slowly beat this into the creamy cod's roe mixture, stirring all the time.

3. Now whip the cream to floppy peaks and in a separate bowl whisk the egg whites until almost stiff. Working quickly, fold the cream into the cod's roe, and then beat in a big spoonful of egg-white to loosen the mix, then gently fold in the rest. Spoon into a serving dish or individual pots and spread level. Chill.

4. Now make the jelly. Pour the fish stock, wine and wine vinegar into the saucepan. Add the chopped shallot and peppercorns. Bring to the boil, stirring occasionally. Boil hard to reduce to about 300 ml (½ pint). Take it off the heat.

5. Pour 3 tablespoons of cold water into a very small saucepan. Sprinkle the gelatine onto the water and leave to swell for 5 minutes. Then very gently heat the gelatine to dissolve it. As it starts to dissolve pour a little of the fish stock mixture into the gelatine and mix it well. Pour into the reduced fish stock and stir to mix. Stir in the chopped herbs, then leave to cool. When cool and beginning to set and go syrupy, pour a thin layer on top of the mousse(s), then chill for 2–3 hours. Serve with thinly sliced brown bread and butter or crisp toasts.

smoked salmon and trout rillettes

Not quite potted salmon, but a delicate mix of smoked trout and smoked salmon. This is a fish version of the French dish usually made with pork or duck that is served with crusty bread and eaten on a picnic. Cooked par-smoked trout and cooked smoked salmon are shredded and mixed with crushed peppercorns and butter. I sometimes pour a layer of melted butter over each one and scatter a few extra peppercorns on top, then chill to set. A perfect, hassle-free starter or picnic pâté.

SERVES 6

4 x 110 g (4 oz) par-smoked trout fillets, skin on
600 ml (1 pint) fish stock or water
3 fresh or dried bay leaves
350 g (12 oz) unsliced smoked salmon (royal fillet), cut into 2.5 cm (1 inch) cubes
350 g (12 oz) unsalted butter, softened
1–2 tablespoons green or pink peppercorns in brine, drained and crushed
fine sea salt

1. Place the trout fillets skin-side-up in a deep frying pan that will just take them, and cover with the fish stock. Add the bay leaves, bring to a simmer and poach for 7 minutes. Remove from the heat and allow to cool in the liquid (the fillets will carry on cooking in the cooling liquid, but remain tender and juicy cooked this way).

2. Melt 40g of the butter in a frying pan and sauté the cubed smoked salmon until just opaque. Cool completely.

3. When cold, remove the cooked trout from the liquid and peel off the skin.

4. Using a fork, shred both the cooked fishes together. Beat the remaining butter until very soft then beat the fish into it with the peppercorns. Taste and season well.

5. Press into individual dishes, level and refrigerate until set and firm. Remove from the fridge 15 minutes before serving to come to room temperature. Serve with melba toast or something equally crunchy – breadsticks are fun.

summer dips

When all our friends are gathered round and catching up over a meal, I love to have these dips to hand, so everyone can tuck in while I cook. Using low-fat fromage frais means that when I serve these with chopped raw salad vegetables even friends on a diet can indulge.

roast smoked salmon and red pesto dip

SERVES ABOUT 12 AS A DIP

200 g (7 oz) roast smoked salmon, flaked
300 g (10 oz) fromage frais or light cream cheese
4 tablespoons bought/prepared red pesto
3 tablespoons chopped sundried tomatoes
3 tablespoons chopped fresh basil
salt and freshly ground black pepper

1. Put the salmon, fromage frais or cream cheese and pesto into a food processor and blend in short bursts until smooth.

2. Scrape out into a bowl and stir in the sun-dried tomatoes and chopped basil. Taste and season with salt and pepper.

3. Serve with crudités or tortilla chips for dipping.

lemon and smoked cod's roe dip

SERVES 4–6 AS A DIP

80 g (3 oz) smoked cod's roe
2 tablespoons fresh lemon juice, or more, to taste
6 tablespoons Greek yoghurt
12 tablespoons good-quality bought mayonnaise
4–5 teaspoons chopped fresh tarragon
a dash of Tabasco (the green Jalapeno one is good with this!)
freshly ground black pepper

1. Scoop the cod's roe out of the skin and beat with a couple of tablespoons of lemon juice until smooth.

2. Now beat in the Greek yoghurt, then the mayonnaise and the tarragon plus a dash of Tabasco.

3. Taste and add extra lemon juice and some black pepper. Delicious with toasted pitta bread or sesame breadsticks.

summer salmon terrine

This is perfect on a cool summer evening as a starter or served cold as part of a buffet or picnic. A very pretty light terrine that can be served warm or cold, but best not served at fridge temperature, as the cold deadens the flavour of the fish.

SERVES 8

200 g (7 oz) smoked salmon, chopped
45 ml (3 tablespoons) dry vermouth
55 g (2 oz) butter
1 medium leek, white part only, finely chopped
750 g (1½ lbs) par-smoked salmon fillets, skinned
juice of 1 lemon
the zest of 2 lemons (reserve the lemons)
300 ml (½ pint) whipping cream, chilled
2 medium egg whites, chilled
3 tablespoons chopped fresh basil
salt and freshly ground black pepper

1. Marinate the smoked salmon for 30 minutes in the dry vermouth and a good twist of pepper.

2. Preheat the oven to Fan 160°C /180°C/350°F/Gas Mark 4. Lightly oil a 1 kg (2 lb) loaf tin and line the base with baking parchment.

3. Melt the butter in a small saucepan and gently fry the chopped leek for 10 minutes until soft and golden, but not browned. Cool.

4. Cut up the par-smoked salmon roughly and place in a food processor with the cooled leek, half the lemon juice, lemon zest, whipping cream and egg whites. Process in short bursts for 1 or 2 minutes until the mixture is smooth (over-processing can lead to the mixture curdling, so keep an eye on it!). Taste and adjust seasoning by adding more lemon juice and pepper – salt only if it needs it.

5. Peel the zested lemons with a knife removing all skin and pith. Slice very thinly and arrange over the base of the loaf tin, overlapping them until the base is covered.

6. Carefully spoon just under half of the creamy salmon mousse over the lemon slices, and level with the back of a spoon.

7. Mix the basil with the chopped smoked salmon and scatter this evenly over the salmon mousse. Spoon the remaining salmon mousse over the chopped smoked salmon in small dollops then spread them out to join them up and cover the chopped smoked salmon completely.

8. Cover with buttered foil and set the loaf tin in a deep roasting tin. Fill with boiling water to come as high up the sides of the loaf tin as possible and bake for about 40 minutes or until a thin-bladed knife inserted into the centre of the terrine comes out clean.

9. When cooked, lift out of the roasting tin and cool until just warm or cold. Invert onto a board and cut into neat slices. Serve warm or cold with a pretty salad, or even a warm potato salad.

accompaniments

tsatziki

SERVES 4

1 cucumber
2 teaspoons salt
200 ml (7 fl oz) Greek yoghurt
1 tablespoon extra virgin olive oil
2 heaped tablespoons freshly
    chopped mint
2 peeled and crushed garlic cloves
lemon juice to taste
salt and freshly ground black pepper

Think hot summer days. This cool and creamy yet tangy cucumber dip, flavoured with garlic, is the perfect complement for all grilled or roasted fish.

1. Grate the unpeeled cucumber into a sieve, sprinkle with the salt, mix and leave for about an hour to drain. Rinse under cold water then squeeze out all the excess liquid and pat dry with kitchen paper.

2. Place in a bowl and stir in the yoghurt, olive oil, mint and garlic. Add fresh lemon juice and seasoning to taste.

67

olive and preserved lemon tapenade

MAKES ENOUGH FOR ABOUT
35 CANAPES

65 g (3½ oz) stoned weight Greek-
    style black olives, chopped
1½ oz whole preserved lemons,
    chopped
2 tablespoons capers in brine,
    drained and chopped
½ garlic clove, peeled and chopped
2 teaspoons fresh thyme, chopped
1 teaspoon paprika
2 tablespoons decent olive oil
freshly ground black pepper

For quick party food, spread toasted crostini with the tapenade and pile on some smoked fish. I immediately feel as if I am in France with all those wonderful Mediterranean tastes and smells.

1. Mix everything together, taste and season.

2. To serve, spoon onto crostini or small toasts topped with smoked halibut or any smoked fish for a truly delicious canapé.

curry butter for kedgeree (or grilled fish)

MAKES 125 g (4 oz)

125 g (4 oz) unsalted butter, softened
2 thin slices fresh ginger, finely
    chopped
1 shallot, finely chopped
1 garlic clove, finely chopped
1 small hot green chilli, seeded and
    finely chopped
1 tablespoon garam masala
1 tablespoon mild curry powder
1 tablespoon fresh lemon juice
1 pinch ground turmeric
salt and freshly ground black
    pepper, to taste

I find this butter really useful for spicing up a dish, be it kedgeree, grilled fish or chicken, or sometimes just melted over a baked potato.

1. For a smooth butter, blend all the ingredients in a food processor.

2. For a pretty textured butter, beat the butter to a cream then mix in all the remaining ingredients.

3. Spoon onto clingfilm into a long, rough sausage shape, roll up clingfilm and twist the ends until firm. Chill for 2 hours and slice as needed or freeze for up to 3 months.

danish rémoulade sauce (remouladesås)

SERVES 4

175 ml (6 fl oz) good-quality
    mayonnaise
4 tablespoons double cream,
    whipped
1½ tablespoons yellow squeezy
    mustard (or Dijon)
½ tablespoon chopped capers
½ tablespoon chopped chives
½ tablespoon chopped parsley
½ tablespoon chopped pickled
    gherkins
few drops Worcestershire sauce or
    some chopped anchovy fillet
salt and freshly ground black pepper

One of the recipes I brought back with me from our time living in Denmark. It is delicious with all smoked fish.

Fold the cream into the mayonnaise, then fold in all the remaining ingredients. Taste and season. Mix all ingredients until well blended.

Rosie's melba toast

TIP

This seems to work best with white sliced bread, but you can experiment with any type of sliced loaf.

1. Preheat the oven to 200°C/400°F/Gas Mark 6.

2. Lightly toast both sides of the bread in a toaster. (Toasting lightly will help the bread curl up in the oven. If over-toasted at this stage, the bread won't curl.)

3. Whilst still hot, cut off the crusts, then split the toast horizontally through the slice of bread, leaving the soft centre.

4. Stack up in a pile, toasted side down. When you have enough, arrange on baking trays and bake for about 5–10 minutes, watching like a hawk, until light golden brown.

5. Remove from the oven and allow to cool. Keep in an airtight container for up to 4 days.

autumn recipes

brandade of smoked haddock and capers

The French make this dish with salt cod, but it works very well with smoked haddock, Arbroath Smokies or even smoked mackerel. It is best served warm with hot toast or with a tomato salad.

450 g (1 lb) piece smoked haddock
450 ml (¾ pint) milk
sprig of fresh thyme
1 bay leaf
8 peppercorns
450 g (1 lb) floury potatoes, peeled and diced
150 ml (¼ pint) good rapeseed or mild olive oil
3 garlic cloves, crushed
2 tablespoons chopped capers
3 tablespoons chopped fresh parsley
3 tablespoons chopped fresh chives
extra oil, for drizzling
crusty bread or melba toast, to serve
salt and freshly ground black pepper

1. Place the smoked haddock in a pan with the milk and enough water to cover, plus the thyme, bay leaf and peppercorns. Bring to the boil, then remove from the heat and allow to cool in the liquid. When cool strain the milk from the fish and reserve.

2. Next, simmer the potatoes in the strained milk for about 20 minutes until completely tender then strain, again reserving the milk. Mash and keep warm.

3. Break up the haddock into flakes and put in a food processor.

4. Heat the oil in a saucepan, add the garlic and cook for a minute, but don't let the garlic brown.

5. Turn on the processor and slowly add the oil in a steady stream until all used up.

6. Scrape the mixture into a bowl and beat in the capers, chives and parsley, then the potato and enough of the reserved milk to give a soft creamy consistency. Season well.

7. Pile into a dish and drizzle with olive oil if you wish before serving with a pile of crusty bread or Rosie's melba toast (see p. 69).

smoked mackerel tart

This tart is just right when you want something a little more substantial than just a salad. To save time I sometimes buy a ready-made pastry case.

SERVES 6–8

FOR THE PASTRY
200g (7 oz) plain flour sifted
125g (4 oz) unsalted butter, diced

FOR THE FILLING
300 ml (½ pint) crème fraîche
2 large eggs
1 bunch of spring onions
180 g (6½ oz) smoked mackerel
salt and freshly ground black pepper

1. Preheat the oven to Fan 170°C/190°C/375°F/Gas Mark 5.

2. Place the flour and butter in a food processor with a pinch of salt and lightly process till the mixture resembles fine breadcrumbs. Put the mixture into a bowl, sprinkle with 3–4 tablespoons cold water and lightly mix till the mixture sticks together. Knead lightly on a lightly floured surface for a few seconds to form a smooth, firm dough – do not overwork. Wrap in clingfilm and chill for an hour or so then roll out to fit a deep 23 cm (9 inch) tart tin. Prick base and chill again.

3. Line the chilled pastry with foil and fill with baking beans. Bake blind for 15 minutes, remove foil and beans and continue to bake for a further 5 minutes.

4. Beat the crème fraîche and eggs together and season.

5. Slice each spring onion in half lengthwise, and then slice into 3–4 cm pieces. Flake the smoked mackerel making sure you take out all the bones. Then pour two-thirds of the egg mix into the pastry case and arrange the onions and mackerel on the egg mix. If there is still room, top up with any remaining egg mix. Season and bake in the oven for 20–30 minutes until just firm.

6. Serve with a mixed green salad or a warm potato and beetroot salad.

hot and spicy grilled trout cutlets

We were having a Hallowe'en party and I wanted to do something different which wouldn't keep me in the kitchen away from all the fun. The par-smoked trout cutlets taste fantastic with this spicy rub.

SERVES 4

4 x 110 g (4 oz) par-smoked trout or
   salmon fillets, skin on

FOR THE SPICY RUB
(keeps well, you may not use it all)

55 g (2 oz) soft brown sugar
1 tablespoon garlic powder
25 g (1 oz) sweet paprika
3 tablespoons freshly ground black
   pepper
1 teaspoon hot chilli seasoning or
   spice mix
½ teaspoon celery or fennel seeds

1. Mix the spice rub ingredients together and rub over the cutlets. Cover and pop in the fridge for 30 minutes.

2. When ready to cook, lay the cutlets, skin side up (to protect the flesh and stop it drying out), onto a grill pan.

3. Place under a hot grill and grill on one side only for 8–10 minutes until golden and cooked through. Turn the cutlets over, baste with the cooking juices and finish off under the grill until crispy (no more than a minute).

4. Delicious served either with baked potatoes and a soured cream and chive sauce or new potatoes and a salad.

> TIP
> Keep any leftover spice rub in a screwtop jar in the cupboard.

smoked sea bass korma

Creamy and mild and a beautiful golden colour . . . you can make this with any cooked smoked fish. It is a wonderful dish to share with friends. Serve with pilau rice if naans are just not enough!

SERVES 4–6

1 pinch saffron threads (about 5 threads)

3.75 cm (1½ inch) piece of fresh ginger, chopped

2 teaspoons mild chilli powder (spice mix with cumin, coriander, chilli and garlic in it)

1 teaspoon ground coriander

¼ teaspoon ground turmeric

seeds from 3 cardamom pods

100 g (3½ oz) unsalted raw cashew nuts

150 ml (¼ pint) Greek yoghurt

1 tablespoon vegetable oil

2 onions, finely chopped

2 garlic cloves, chopped

350–450 g (12 oz–1 lb) smoked sea bass (or other smoked fish), torn into large pieces

55 g (2 oz) flaked almonds, toasted

extra Greek yoghurt, fresh coriander leaves, and warm naan bread, to serve

1. Put the saffron into a small bowl and pour in 400 ml (14 fl oz) boiling water. Set aside to infuse for 10 minutes.

2. Put the ginger, chilli spice mix, coriander, turmeric, cardamom, cashew nuts and yoghurt into a food processor and process until the mixture becomes a smooth paste.

3. Heat the oil in a large frying pan and cook the onions and garlic for 7–10 minutes, or until very soft but not coloured. Add the spice paste and cook over a gentle heat for 2–3 minutes.

4. Pour in the saffron water and stir well. Bring to the boil over a gentle heat and simmer for 5–10 minutes until thickened and creamy, adding a little extra water if needed.

5. Season to taste – but be careful of the salt as the fish could be salty. Add the fish to the hot sauce and simmer for 1 minute.

6. Serve sprinkled with the toasted almonds, with extra yoghurt, coriander leaves, and naan bread.

> **TIP**
> If the sauce is too thin, add 1 teaspoon cornflour slaked in 2–3 table-spoons milk and simmer for 1 minute *before* you add the fish.

kipper hash with tarragon butter eggs

Robert loves making this when home alone as it is perfect bachelor food. A must for kipper lovers and perfect for a lazy brunch. I've also made this with Arbroath Smokies with equal success.

SERVES 4

FOR THE HASH

about 700g (1½ lbs) floury potatoes
350 g (12 oz) boned kipper fillets
  (weight without bones)
1 egg
1 tablespoon sweet chilli sauce
1 onion, grated
1 garlic clove, finely chopped
1 large green chilli, seeded and
  chopped
1 tablespoon finely chopped fresh
  parsley
125 g (4 oz) unsalted butter
freshly ground black pepper

FOR THE TARRAGON EGGS

4 large eggs
a splash of tarragon vinegar
1–2 tablespoons chopped fresh
  tarragon

1. Peel and boil the potatoes until just cooked. Drain well and leave to steam for 5 minutes.

2. Using a fork, mash half of the potatoes in a large bowl then add the remaining potatoes, flaked kipper fillets, egg, chilli sauce, onion, garlic, fresh chilli and parsley. Season generously with pepper and mix well. Chill for at least 2 hours. (This can be done the night before if you want to serve it for breakfast/brunch.)

3. Preheat the oven to Fan 180°C/200°C/400°F/Gas Mark 6.

4. Heat a large heavy non-stick frying pan (that can go in the oven) over a medium/high heat. Add half the butter and when the butter is melted and stops foaming, add the hash mixture and cook briskly, stirring, for 30 seconds. Using a spatula, press the mixture down into a cake the size of the pan. Cook for about 3 minutes, shaking the pan occasionally, until the hash begins to brown on the underside.

5. Reduce the heat to medium and continue cooking, shaking the pan to loosen the hash occasionally, until the underside is browned and crusty, then finish cooking in the oven for 10 minutes.

6. Fry the eggs in the remaining butter according to taste, then sprinkle with chopped tarragon and a dash of tarragon vinegar, salt and pepper.

7. To serve, cut the hash cake into wedges and serve with the fried eggs, spooning any remaining butter over.

> **TIP**
> Inverawe kippers are already split open, with the backbone exposed. Remove the backbone gently by using a knife, starting under the tail to ease the bone upwards towards the head and lift off. Any stray bones can be removed with tweezers.

smoked haddock soufflé baked in a mushroom

This is such a comforting kitchen supper – the smoky fish and the mushrooms give a real flavour of autumn. Serve with light greens and French bread.

SERVES 6 AS A STARTER

400 g (14 oz) skinless undyed smoked haddock fillets
about 300 ml (½ pint) milk
6 very large open-cup mushrooms (sometimes known as Portobello mushrooms)
55 g (2 oz) butter plus extra melted butter, for brushing
40 g (1½ oz) plain flour
3 tablespoons freshly grated Parmesan
2 tablespoons grated cheddar or Gruyère cheese
2 teaspoons Dijon mustard
2 medium egg yolks
6 medium egg whites
salt and freshly ground black pepper

1. Preheat the oven to Fan 170°C/190°C/375°F/Gas Mark 5.

2. Place the haddock in a shallow ovenproof dish and cover with milk, cover with a lid or foil and bake in the oven for 20 minutes until just cooked.

3. Meanwhile place the mushrooms open-side up on a buttered baking tray, brush with melted butter, season well and place in the oven with the fish. Bake the mushrooms for 7–10 minutes (until half-cooked) then remove from the oven and set aside to cool slightly.

4. Take the fish out of the oven and allow to cool a little. As soon as the fish is cool enough to handle, lift it out of the milk. Remove any stray bones and flake the fish, set aside. Strain the milk into a jug and reserve.

5. In a medium saucepan, melt the 55 g (2 oz) butter and add the flour, cook, stirring until very lightly brown and toasted. Gradually add 250 ml (8 fl oz) of the strained milk, whisking all the time and continue to cook gently until thick.

6. Sprinkle the mushrooms with half the Parmesan.

7. Beat the cheddar, mustard and egg yolks into the sauce then fold in the flaked haddock and transfer to a large bowl. Season with black pepper and salt if it needs it.

8. In a separate bowl, whisk the egg whites with a pinch of salt to soft peaks. Mix about a third of the egg whites into the haddock mixture to loosen it, then lightly fold in the rest.

9. Fill each mushroom with 2 large tablespoons of the mixture, sprinkle with the remaining Parmesan and bake for 10–12 minutes until puffed and browned. Serve immediately.

smoked salmon, butternut squash and gorgonzola tart

This is gorgeous – made really special by the Gorgonzola. It's almost like a pizza, but crisper and quicker to make. A great quick supper dish and perfect for Hallowe'en parties.

SERVES 4

2 small heads of garlic
900 g (2 lb) butternut squash, peeled, seeded and diced
2 tablespoons olive oil, plus extra for drizzling
1 onion, finely chopped
10 sage leaves, chopped
75 g (3 oz) freshly grated Parmesan
375 g packet ready-rolled puff pastry sheet
150 g (5 oz) Gorgonzola, diced
175 g (6 oz) smoked salmon trimmings, diced
2–3 tablespoons chopped fresh spring onions or chives

1. Preheat oven to Fan 180°C/200°C/400°F/Gas Mark 6.

2. Wrap the bulbs of garlic in foil and roast in the oven for 20 minutes. Set aside.

3. Meanwhile, heat the olive oil in a large saucepan, fry the onion for 10 minutes over a medium heat until just starting to brown. Add the sage leaves and the butternut squash, cover with a lid and cook for about 15 minutes until tender. Mash the squash roughly, squeeze in half of the roasted garlic cloves, then stir in the Parmesan. Season to taste.

4. Unroll the puff pastry, roll out a little bit thinner and put onto a large, non-stick baking tray or greased baking tray. Prick all over with a fork then spread with the butternut squash. Bake for 10 minutes then scatter the diced Gorgonzola on top and bake for another 10 minutes until the pastry has risen and is golden brown. Finally top with the smoked salmon and the remaining roasted garlic cloves and return to the oven for 3 minutes.

5. Remove from the oven, drizzle with a little olive oil and sprinkle with the spring onions or chives before serving with a fresh mixed leaf salad.

> TIP
> This is equally good made with Dolcelatte.

smoked venison and red wine risotto

It may seem unusual to use game in a risotto but the combination of robust flavours in this dish work wonderfully together. It has Robert's total approval.

SERVES 6

300 g (10 oz) smoked venison
2 fresh bay leaves
large sprig of fresh thyme
4 juniper berries, lightly crushed
about 1.5 litres (2½ pints) hot game,
    beef or chicken stock
125 g (4 oz) butter
1 medium onion, finely chopped
1 medium carrot, finely chopped
1 celery stick, finely chopped
55g (2 oz) pancetta or bacon
    lardons, finely chopped
500 g (1 lb) Italian risotto rice
300 ml (½ pint) red wine (such as
    Chianti)
1 tablespoon chopped fresh thyme
75 g (3 oz) freshly grated Parmesan
salt and freshly ground black pepper
mixed chopped fresh parsley and
    thyme, to garnish

1. Dice or shred the smoked venison and set aside.

2. Add the bay leaves, thyme and juniper berries to the stock and simmer for 10 minutes, then strain the stock into a pan and keep at simmering point on the top of the stove/hob while you make the risotto.

3. Melt half the butter in a medium heavy-based saucepan and add the onion, carrot and celery (this is a *soffritto* in Italian). Cook gently (sweat) for 10 minutes until soft and golden but not coloured.

4. Add the pancetta and half the smoked venison and cook for another 5 minutes, but do not let it colour and harden. Stir in the rice until well-coated with butter, heated through and beginning to smell 'toasted'. Pour in the wine and add the thyme, bring to the boil and boil hard to reduce by half – this will concentrate the flavour and remove the raw taste of alcohol.

5. Begin to add the stock a large ladleful at a time, stirring gently until each ladleful is absorbed into the rice. The rice should always be at a gentle simmer. Continue in this way until the rice is tender and creamy, but the grains still firm. (This should take between 15 and 20 minutes depending on the type of rice used.) Taste and season well with salt and freshly ground black pepper and beat in the remaining butter and Parmesan.

6. Cover and rest for a couple of minutes then serve immediately with the remaining venison piled on top, sprinkled with chopped parsley and thyme.

88

smoked salmon fishballs with linguine and tomato sauce

A healthy alternative to meatballs served with a real tomato sauce made from scratch. These are the grandchildren's favourite: they're tasty, take minutes to cook and the little ones can roll their sleeves up and help make the fishballs themselves.

SERVES 4–6

450 g (1 lb) par-smoked salmon
   cutlets, skinned
55 g (2 oz) stale white breadcrumbs
about 4 tablespoons milk
2 tablespoons pine nuts
2 tablespoon chopped capers
2 tablespoons chopped fresh parsley
2 tablespoons grated Parmesan or
   Pecorino cheese
1 medium egg, beaten
a little flour, to coat
olive oil, for frying

FOR THE TOMATO SAUCE
8 tablespoons olive oil
2 garlic cloves, chopped
1 teaspoon dried oregano
two 400 g cans chopped tomatoes
sea salt and freshly ground black
   pepper

450 g (1 lb) dried linguine

1. Chop the salmon into very, very small pieces. This is better done by hand rather than in a food processor as it gives the fish a much better texture.

2. Soak the breadcrumbs in the milk until soft. Squeeze out the excess liquid and mix the crumbs with the fish. Add the pine nuts, capers, parsley, cheese, egg and seasoning (watch the salt).

3. Work these ingredients together well with your hands or mixer until they are thoroughly amalgamated, and then shape into little balls. The easiest way to do this is to divide the mixture into 24 equal pieces and then roll each one into a ball. (If you wash your hands before beginning, and keep a bowl of water on the side to wet your hands from time to time you will find the mixture won't stick to them!) Place on a baking sheet then cover and chill for 30 minutes to firm them up.

4. Meanwhile, make the sauce. Heat the oil in a large shallow pan – almost to smoking point (a wok is good for this). Stand back as it will splutter, and add the chopped garlic, oregano and tomatoes. Cook over a fierce heat for 5 to 8 minutes or until the sauce is thick and glossy, then taste and season.

5. Sprinkle some flour onto a large plate and dip the fishballs into the flour making sure they are well coated. Tap off the excess and set on a tray.

6. Heat a little oil in a frying pan and quickly brown the fishballs all over. Pour the tomato sauce over the fishballs, bring to the boil then turn down the heat and simmer them for 5–10 minutes until cooked.

7. While the fishballs are cooking, cook the linguine according to the manufacturer's instructions. Drain well and serve with the fishballs and sauce.

smoked fish lasagne

Another twist on a classic Italian dish and perfect for when the family invades. This is a luscious, creamy lasagne packed with dense bites of smoked fish and the burst of juicy tomatoes. I used a mixture of haddock and roast smoked salmon but you can make it with whatever you like best.

SERVES 4

250 g (9 oz) pack fresh egg lasagne sheets (about 9 sheets in all)
75 g (3 oz) butter
225 g (8 oz) chopped or sliced mushrooms
225 g (8 oz) grated mild cheddar cheese
225 g (8 oz) cherry tomatoes, halved
225 g (8 oz) flaked smoked fish (of any sort)

FOR THE SAUCE

40 g (1½ oz) plain flour
300 ml (½ pint) milk, warmed
100 g (3½ oz) Boursin cheese
150 ml (¼ pint) double cream
freshly ground black pepper

> **TIP**
> If you like a firmer lasagne with more layers of pasta, then add a layer between each ingredient. You will need more lasagne of course.

1. Melt 20 g (1 oz) of the butter in a saucepan, add the sliced mushrooms, season with pepper and cook for 5 minutes until soft and all the moisture has evaporated. Set aside.

2. Melt the remaining 55 g (2 oz) butter, add the flour and whisk over a gentle heat until smooth, then remove from the heat and slowly add the warm milk to create a smooth sauce. Return it to the heat, bring to the boil whisking all the time until the sauce thickens, then reduce the heat and cook for 1–2 minutes, continue stirring. Finally take it off the heat and stir in the Boursin cheese and double cream.

To assemble the lasagne

1. Put a layer of sauce over the base of a 25 cm x 18 cm (10 inch x 7 inch) deep rectangular ovenproof dish. Sprinkle with a quarter of the cheddar cheese. Place lasagne sheets on top to cover (approx. 3). Cover with half of the tomatoes, half of the cooked mushrooms and half the flaked smoked fish. Spoon over a further thin layer of sauce, and sprinkle with another quarter of the cheddar cheese. Lay 3 more lasagne sheets on top to cover. Cover with the remaining tomatoes, cooked mushrooms and flaked smoked fish. Spoon over a further thin layer of sauce and sprinkle half the remaining cheddar cheese. Top with 3 more lasagne sheets (if room in the dish), spoon over any remaining sauce and sprinkle with the remaining cheddar cheese. This will sit happily in the fridge for 2–3 hours.

2. Bake in a preheated oven for about 25 minutes at Fan 170°C/190°C/375°F/Gas Mark 5 until the cheese begins to brown and then place it under the grill for 5 minutes more if you want a crispy golden top.

92

flavoured vodkas

Some years ago I was at a dinner party given by some Swedish friends who always make their own flavoured vodka. They served it with Inverawe smoked salmon in my honour – and seriously good it was too! Why not have some fun trying out these delicious flavours and then experiment with your own. The method will be much the same for any kind, although infusion times can vary. Always use a clean preserving jar with a tight-fitting lid, leave to infuse in a dark room and when ready strain into a clean glass bottle, which must also have a tight-fitting lid.

black pepper vodka

100 g (3½ oz) whole black
   peppercorns, roughly crushed
1 x 70 cl bottle vodka
infusion time 2–4 weeks

1. Put the crushed peppercorns into a clean glass preserving jar with a tight-fitting lid and pour in the vodka. Leave to steep for between 2 and 4 weeks in a dark place at room temperature, 18°–20°C (64°–68°F). Shake lightly and taste from time to time.

2. When ready strain and filter into a clean glass bottle or jar with a tight-fitting lid. Keep the finished vodka bottle tightly closed and in a dark place. Serve after it has settled for a couple of days, though it gets even better after ageing for a while in a dark place at room temperature.

dill vodka

fresh dill leaves/fronds (a good
   bunch)
1 x 70 cl bottle vodka
infusion time 5–7 days

1. You can use leaves/fronds, flowers, seeds, and even the whole umbels from the dill plant.

2. If buying fresh dill make sure the plant is really fresh and undamaged. Handle the plant with care and use the leaves as soon as possible to get the most flavour and aroma into the vodka. Rinse the fresh dill leaves carefully – but only if really necessary – and dry carefully on kitchen paper.

3. Fill the preserving jar one-third full of dill leaves, pour on the vodka, and leave to infuse for 5–7 days. Strain, filter and bottle as above, and then serve after it has settled for a couple of days. Dill vodka doesn't keep well at room temperature, so keep the bottle in the freezer and serve it iced.

94

lemon vodka

6 lemons (preferably unwaxed)
1 x 70 cl bottle vodka
infusion time 2-4 days

1. Scrub the lemons thoroughly to remove dirt or any chemical residue and wax. Dry and peel them thinly with a potato peeler or zester to remove the yellow zest, leaving the bitter white pith behind.

2. Fill the clean preserving jar with the lemon zest, add the vodka, and allow to infuse for 2 to 4 days. Shake lightly and taste it from time to time – it must not get bitter. Strain and filter into a clean bottle as above and store at room temperature.

3. Serve lemon vodka at room temperature in suitable glasses. (It gets even better if kept for a month or so before serving.)

cucumber vodka

1 large cucumber
1 x 70 cl bottle of vodka
infusion time 4–5 days

1. Scrub the cucumber in warm soapy water to rid it of any wax or preservatives and dry. Slice into thick rounds, leaving the skin on.

2. Follow the method as before, filling the preserving jar with the cucumber slices and then adding the vodka. Infuse for 4 to 5 days, then strain and bottle.

3. Cucumber vodka has a cool, clean flavour and is particularly good with smoked salmon. It is also very good served chilled and mixed with some dill vodka.

95

winter recipes

roast smoked salmon and rice fishcakes

These are deliciously light and crumbly and although they are easier to handle if coated in flour before frying, they taste even better uncoated.

SERVES 4 (MAKES ABOUT 16)

55 g (2 oz) butter
½ teaspoon ground turmeric
a pinch of ground coriander
1 medium onion, finely chopped
1 garlic clove, crushed (optional)
175 g (6 oz) Thai jasmine rice
3 tablespoons chopped fresh parsley
    or coriander
1 egg yolk
2 tablespoons natural yoghurt
200 g (7 oz) roast smoked salmon,
    flaked and checked for bones
a good squeeze of lemon juice
salt and freshly ground black pepper
seasoned flour for coating (optional)
sunflower oil, for frying
lemon wedges, to serve

1. Melt the butter and add the spices and onion and garlic. Cook over a moderate heat for 5 minutes. Add the rice, stir well to coat then add 350 ml (12 fl oz) boiling water. Cover and simmer for 15 minutes, until all the water is absorbed, then turn off the heat, keep covered and leave to swell for 5 minutes.

2. Tip the rice into a bowl and fork up. While the rice is still hot, beat the egg yolk with the yoghurt and chopped herbs and mix into the rice. Next mix in the flaked salmon and season with salt, pepper and lemon juice. Shape into about 16 fish cakes. Roll in seasoned flour and place in the fridge for at least 1 hour to firm up.

3. Heat a couple of tablespoons of sunflower oil in a non-stick frying pan and fry the fishcakes in batches for about 2–3 minutes on each side or until golden brown and hot. Serve immediately with lemon wedges.

walnut and herb crusted par-smoked trout cutlets with watercress tartare sauce

This is a brilliantly versatile recipe that you could easily do with fresh salmon, cod or mackerel cutlets. The watercress tartare is crunchy, herby and creamy. A taste sensation.

SERVES 4

FOR THE WATERCRESS TARTARE SAUCE
300 ml (½ pint) bought mayonnaise
55 g (2 oz) watercress leaves, blanched, squeezed dry and very finely chopped
1 teaspoon finely chopped fresh tarragon
2 tablespoons chopped fresh parsley
1 tablespoon chopped capers
2 tablespoons chopped gherkins

FOR THE TROUT CRUST
1 tablespoon mixed red, green and white dry peppercorns
4 x 110 g (4 oz) par-smoked trout fillets, with skin
125 g (4½ oz) granary breadcrumbs
75 g (3 oz) shelled walnuts, chopped
8 tablespoons mixed chopped fresh herbs (parsley, dill, coriander, chives)
finely grated zest of 1 orange
freshly grated nutmeg
125 g (4 oz) butter, melted
1 egg yolk, beaten
salt and freshly ground black pepper
extra watercress and lemon wedges, to serve

1. Preheat the oven to Fan 180°C/200°C/400°F/Gas Mark 6.

2. First make the tartare sauce by beating the watercress into the mayonnaise then folding in all the remaining ingredients. Taste, season and chill until needed.

3. Pound the peppercorns in a pestle and mortar. Rub this mixture all over the flesh side of the cutlets. Then lay them skin-side down in a baking dish.

4. Mix the breadcrumbs with the walnuts, herbs, orange zest, and lots of nutmeg.

5. Melt the butter in a frying pan, and when foaming, stir in the breadcrumb mixture. Cook over a high heat until the butter is absorbed and the breadcrumbs are just beginning to toast and brown. Season well.

6. Brush the peppered cutlets with egg yolk and press on the walnut and bread-crumb mixture.

7. Bake for 15–20 minutes until the fish is opaque and the crumbs crisp. Serve with the watercress tartare sauce and lemon wedges.

celeriac and smoked haddock gratin

To speed up the cooking process and so as not to overcook the haddock, microwave the potato, celeriac and cream mixture on High for about 10 minutes until almost cooked, then use to layer the dish.

SERVES 6

55 g (2 oz) butter
1 medium onion, finely chopped
350 g (12 oz) smoked haddock,
   skinned and cut into large chunks
4 tablespoons chopped fresh parsley
450 g (1 lb) celeriac, peeled
750 g (1½ lbs) Rooster or King
   Edward potatoes, peeled
300 ml (½ pint) double cream
4 tablespoons freshly grated
   cheddar or Parmesan
salt and freshly ground black pepper

1. Preheat the oven to Fan 170°C/190°C/375°F/Gas Mark 5.

2. Melt the butter and cook the onions until soft and beginning to brown. Remove from heat and stir in the haddock, parsley, and salt and pepper to taste.

3. Slice the celeriac and the potatoes on a mandoline slicer or with the slicing blade in a food processor.

4. Pour the cream and salt and pepper to taste into the sliced potato and celeriac then tip the whole lot into a wide shallow saucepan and simmer for 20 minutes or microwave on High for about 10 minutes, until almost cooked through.

5. Arrange half of this mixture in a buttered baking dish. Arrange the haddock on top, then cover with the remaining potato mix. Pour over any remaining cream and sprinkle with the cheese. Bake for about 30 minutes until cooked golden and bubbling. Allow to stand for 10 minutes before serving with buttered broccoli or winter greens.

smoked salmon puffs

A much-loved family favourite. Just pile these high with the fresh herb sauce alongside and watch them disappear. If you prefer not to fry the little choux balls in hot oil then just pop them in the oven until golden instead.

SERVES 6–8 AS A STARTER
(MAKES ABOUT 30)

FOR THE FRESH HERB SAUCE
55 g (2 oz) mixed fresh herb leaves
   (e.g. basil, dill, coriander, parsley)
8 tablespoons good quality
   mayonnaise
finely grated zest of 1 large lemon
fresh lemon juice, to taste

FOR THE CHOUX PASTRY
85 g (3¼ oz) butter, cubed
125 g (4 oz) plain flour, sifted
3 medium eggs, beaten
2 tablespoons freshly grated
   Parmesan cheese
100 g (3½ oz) smoked salmon, finely
   chopped
sweet paprika, to dust
a pinch of salt

1. First make the herb sauce. Throw the herbs into boiling water for about 10 seconds, then drain and refresh in a bowl of cold water. Drain the herbs, pat dry on kitchen paper and put into a bowl with the grated lemon zest, mayonnaise and a dash of lemon juice. Blitz until smooth using a hand blender. Cover and chill in the fridge for about 30 minutes for the flavours to infuse. Season with salt, pepper and extra lemon juice if necessary before serving.

2. To make the puffs, put the butter and 225 ml (8 fl oz) water together in a heavy saucepan. Bring slowly to the boil so that by the time the water boils, the butter is completely melted. Immediately the mixture is boiling really fast, tip in the flour, remove from the heat and working quickly beat the mixture hard with a wooden spoon – it will soon become thick and smooth and leave the sides of the pan.

3. When the mixture has cooled slightly (a couple of minutes), beat in the eggs a little at a time, until it is soft, shiny and smooth. It should be of dropping consistency – not too runny. ('Dropping consistency' means that the mixture will fall off a spoon reluctantly and all in a blob. If it runs off, it is too soft.) Beat in the Parmesan then the chopped smoked salmon.

4. Place heaped teaspoons of the mixture onto a well-oiled baking sheet. Heat a deep fat fryer to 170°C (340°F). Lift the teaspoons of choux paste one at a time with the end of a metal palette knife or metal spoon dipped into the hot oil to prevent it sticking. Slide the choux mounds gently into the hot oil. Don't fill too full – cook 6–8 at a time, allowing them to puff up.

5. Cook for 4–6 minutes until golden, puffed up and firm, stirring once or twice. Drain well on kitchen paper and dust with paprika and salt. Keep warm in a low oven with the door ajar to prevent them becoming soft while you cook the others. Serve with the herb sauce for dipping into.

kipper kedgeree

Although I've included this as a winter recipe, kedgeree is one of those great brunch dishes that our family enjoys regardless of the season. Using kippers rather than the traditional smoked haddock is my way of trying to create a new variation of a much-loved favourite.

SERVES 4–6

2–3 whole kippers, about 200 g (7 oz) each with head
55 g (2 oz) butter, plus extra for grilling
225 g (8 oz) cherry or mini plum tomatoes
2 tablespoons olive oil
350 g (12 oz) quick-cook mixed wild and long grain rice
2 teaspoons mild curry powder
1 teaspoon turmeric
1 teaspoon cumin seeds (optional)
1 teaspoon fennel seeds (optional)
1–2 garlic cloves, crushed
1 bag watercress, washed and roughly chopped
2–3 hard-boiled eggs, quartered
salt and freshly ground black pepper

1. Pre-heat the grill to High and the oven to Fan 180°C/200°C/400°F/Gas Mark 6.

2. Lay the kippers in a foil-lined grill pan. Put a few knobs of butter on top of the kippers and grill for 4 to 6 minutes, until cooked through. Cool slightly then remove the skin and bones and flake while still warm. Set aside.

3. Put the tomatoes into a baking dish and toss with 2 tablespoons olive oil. Season with salt and pepper, then bake in the oven for 10 minutes. Remove when cooked and set aside.

4. Cook the rice according to the manufacturer's instructions, drain well.

5. Meanwhile, melt the butter in a large frying pan, add the curry powder, turmeric and spices (if using) then add the garlic and cook over a low heat for 1 minute. Stir in the cooked rice to coat, then gently stir in the kippers, tomatoes and chopped watercress. Taste and season. Serve topped with the quartered boiled eggs.

> **TIP**
> To skin and bone the kippers, pick up the backbone just below the head, and as you gently tug it up and away from the fillet, the thinner bones should lift up too. Pick out any stubborn ones, then break the fillet into small pieces. Discard the skin and bones.

106

Inverawe blinis

These are my ultimate festive party special. They are so easy to make and never fail to look spectacular. Top with classic smoked salmon and crème fraîche before sprinkling with little bubble bursts of trout caviar.

SERVES 8 (MAKES ABOUT 24)

225 g (8 oz) wholewheat, buckwheat
　or rye flour
225 g (8 oz) plain flour
½ teaspoon salt
2 teaspoons sugar
25 g (1 oz) active dried yeast
700 ml (1¼ pints) warm milk
3 medium eggs, beaten
1 tablespoon melted butter
extra butter, for cooking

TO SERVE
350 g (12 oz) smoked salmon
300 ml (½ pint) crème fraîche
2 x 50 g (1½ oz) jars trout caviar

1. Sift the two flours together into a warm dry mixing bowl and add the salt.

2. Whisk the sugar and yeast into the warm milk (should just be hot enough so you can put your finger in for 20 seconds comfortably), mix well and leave for 10 minutes until frothy. Pour into the flour along with the beaten eggs and melted butter. Gradually mix to a batter, bringing in the surrounding flour. Beat well until smooth. Place the bowl inside a plastic carrier bag and tie the handles together to enclose. Leave in a warm place for 2 hours until risen and bubbly.

3. Grease a girdle or heavy frying pan lightly with butter. Heat it gently over steady heat.

4. When the girdle is hot pour spoonfuls of the batter onto the surface to make small pancakes. When bubbles rise and the surface begins to look cooked around the edges, turn over and cook the other side to a light brown. Keep the blinis warm wrapped in a clean tea cloth.

5. Serve topped with smoked salmon, crème fraîche, trout caviar, lemon and black pepper.

109

smoked salmon tartare with wasabi sabayon

I tasted this unusual savoury sabayon sauce on a trip to New York in a wonderful restaurant called Aquavit, and thought it would be just perfect with our smoked salmon… and it is! It looks stunning drizzled around the little mounds of tartare, acting as a perfect foil to its clean fresh flavour, adding a bit of zing. Wasabi powder is available in most large super-markets now, but if you can't find it, use wasabi paste or even creamed horseradish in its place.

SERVES 4

FOR THE PICKLED CUCUMBER
1 medium cucumber, peeled and
    coarsely grated
3 tablespoons rice or white wine
    vinegar
1 teaspoon caster sugar

FOR THE SMOKED SALMON TARTARE
250 g (9 oz) thick smoked salmon
    fillet, skinned (royal fillet)
2 tablespoons each finely chopped
    dill, chives, gherkins and capers
2 teaspoons finely grated lemon
    zest
freshly ground black pepper

FOR THE WASABI SABAYON
4 large egg yolks
125 ml (4 fl oz) dry vermouth
50 ml (2 fl oz) fresh lime juice
2 tablespoons white wine vinegar
2–3 teaspoons wasabi powder
    (Japanese horseradish powder –
    very strong!)
olive oil, to serve

1. Put all pickled cucumber ingredients into a bowl and mix well. Season, cover, place in fridge for 4–6 hours or overnight.

2. Finely dice the salmon and place in a mixing bowl with the dill, chives, gherkins, capers and lemon zest. Season with freshly ground black pepper, stir to mix well (this can be prepared up to a day in advance and kept in the fridge until ready to serve).

3. To make the sabayon, whisk the egg yolks, vermouth, lime juice, and vinegar in a heatproof bowl until well blended. Set in the top of a double boiler (i.e. set over a pan of simmering water – the water must not touch the base of the bowl. Pyrex or a pudding basin is good for this). Whisk constantly using an electric whisk (or by hand if feeling strong) over the heat until the sabayon is thick and foamy, with a slight sheen, about 10 minutes.

4. Whisk in the wasabi powder, taste and season with salt. Turn off the heat but keep the sabayon warm over the hot water until ready to serve.

5. To serve, drain the cucumber in a sieve. Place a 10 cm (4 inch) cook's ring in the centre of each serving plate and half-fill with the cucumber mixture. Press the mixture down firmly using the back of a spoon. Top with the smoked salmon tartare mixture, again pressing down with the back of a spoon. Carefully remove the rings and serve with a drizzle of wasabi sabayon. Drizzle a little olive oil around each portion and serve immediately.

110

cream of artichoke and smoked salmon soup

This smooth and delicate soup is a sophisticated winter warmer. Pure liquid velvet and such a pretty colour.

SERVES 8

900 g (2 lb) Jerusalem artichokes
juice of half a lemon
55 g (2 oz) butter
225 g (8 oz) onions, thinly sliced
1.5 litres (2½ pints) boiling water or
   vegetable stock
100 g (3½ oz) sliced smoked salmon,
   chopped
salt and freshly ground black pepper
chopped fresh chives or chopped
   parsley, to garnish
crème fraîche, to serve

1. Peel the artichokes with a potato peeler, then place immediately into a bowl of cold water with a squeeze of lemon juice (to prevent them turning brown).

2. Heat a large saucepan and add the butter – as soon as it starts to foam, stir in the onions. Reduce the heat and cook for 10 minutes until soft. While you're waiting for the onions to soften, quickly grate or chop the artichokes. Add them to the onions, season well with black pepper and add the boiling water or vegetable stock. Bring back to the boil before reducing to a simmer and cook, covered, for 20 minutes or more until the artichoke is meltingly tender.

3. Pour into a liquidiser and add the smoked salmon. Liquidise until smooth, taste and check the seasoning – you may have to add a squeeze more lemon juice too.

4. Serve immediately with a dollop of crème fraîche and a sprinkling of chives or parsley.

113

roast smoked salmon cobbler

To get ahead, make the cobbler 'scones' beforehand and freeze them, ready to pop on top of the sauce and bake. The filling can be made a day ahead in the dish, covered and chilled.

SERVES 6

400 g (14 oz) roast smoked salmon, flaked

FOR THE SAUCE
55 g (2 oz) butter
55 g (2 oz) plain flour
600 ml (1 pint) milk or milk and fish stock, mixed
450 g (1 lb) frozen leaf spinach, thawed or 900 g (2 lbs) fresh spinach, trimmed and washed
3 medium leeks, trimmed and washed
2–3 tablespoons olive oil
125 g (4 oz) frozen peas

FOR THE COBBLER DOUGH
75 g (3 oz) butter
about 350 g (12 oz) self-raising flour, plus extra for sprinkling
3 tablespoons chopped fresh herbs (parsley, dill, chives)
200 ml (⅓ pint) milk plus extra for brushing
salt and freshly ground black pepper

1. Preheat the oven to Fan 180°C/200°C/400°F/Gas Mark 6.

2. To make the sauce, melt the butter in a heavy saucepan and stir in the flour. Cook, stirring for 1 minute. Remove the pan from the heat. Pour in the milk and whisk well. Return to the heat and slowly bring to the boil, stirring or whisking well all the time. Simmer for 2 minutes. Season well with salt and freshly ground black pepper.

3. Squeeze most of the moisture from the spinach, chop and scatter over the base of a shallow ovenproof dish. Slice the leeks thickly then heat the olive oil in a large frying pan, add the leeks and cook for about 5 minutes, stirring occasionally until they begin to soften. Stir in the peas and then spoon the mixture over the spinach. Cover with a layer of flaked roast smoked salmon and spread the sauce evenly over the top. Set aside.

4. To make the cobbler dough, rub the butter into the flour until it resembles rough breadcrumbs and add a pinch of salt. Stir in the herbs then pour in the milk and stir it together with a blunt table knife until it forms a sticky lump. Tip out onto a floured work surface and knead very lightly until smooth. Working quickly, roll out to a thickness of about 1.25 cm (½ inch) and cut into rounds, squares, triangles or diamonds. Arrange and overlap the cobblers on top of the filling, around the edge of the dish. Brush them with milk (or beaten egg for a shiny finish) then set the dish on an oven tray and slide into the oven to bake for 30–35 minutes until the cobblers are risen and golden brown and the filling bubbling hot (if they begin to brown too much, cover loosely with kitchen foil).

5. Allow to cool for 10 minutes before serving with some extra buttered vegetables – no need for potatoes!

smoked salmon and avocado mousse

This is a dish for a special occasion or for showing off! It will take a little care to prepare, but once it's done it looks and tastes wonderful. I layer this up in individual moulds if I am feeling particularly creative and have the time, although you can make it in one large dish if you prefer.

SERVES ABOUT 6

225 g (8 oz) thinly sliced smoked salmon
225 g (8 oz) cream cheese, softened
240 ml (8 fl oz) soured cream
1 teaspoon Tabasco (or less!)
2 tablespoons fresh lemon juice
1 teaspoon powdered gelatine
75 g (2½ oz) finely chopped spring onions
1 large ripe avocado, stoned, peeled and thinly sliced
2 x 50g (1¾ oz) jars trout caviar
salt and freshly ground black pepper

1. Chop half of the salmon finely and set aside. Chop the other half into bite-size pieces and set aside.

2. Using an electric hand-mixer, beat the cream cheese and soured cream together until creamy and well combined. Beat in the Tabasco and season to taste.

3. Mix the lemon juice with the gelatine in a small bowl, then microwave on High for a few seconds to dissolve it. Repeat until completely dissolved, then beat into the cream cheese mix. Fold in the finely chopped half of the smoked salmon and the chopped spring onions.

4. Stone, peel and thinly slice the avocado. Now you are ready to assemble the dish.

5. First put a layer of the bite-size salmon pieces into the bottom of a wide glass dish, using about a third of the fish in total. Cover with a layer of the creamy mix, using up about half of the quantity. Next add a layer of sliced avocado, using about half of it. Gently dot this layer with about half of the trout caviar. Then add another layer of salmon, using another third of the pieces, followed by the remaining half of the creamy mix. Finally arrange the rest of the sliced avocado evenly over the mix and then top with the remaining bite-size pieces of smoked salmon, and a generous helping of trout caviar to finish.

6. Cover the dish with clingfilm and chill for about 3 hours until firm. If you like, scatter some microgreens over the top and serve with crunchy crostini toasts or curly melba toast (see p. 69).

7. This dish can be made in one big glass serving dish or small individual glasses.

arbroath smokie bubble and squeak with easy hollandaise sauce

This makes the best Boxing Day breakfast. It's an ideal start to the day before a good, long walk blows away all the cobwebs from the previous day's excesses. The fact that it uses up all the leftover brussels sprouts from the day before as well is an added bonus!

SERVES 4

400 g (14 oz) fresh or cooked
  brussels sprouts
1 onion, sliced
butter, for frying
4 bacon rashers, diced
400 g (14 oz) cooked mashed
  potatoes or leftover roast
  potatoes
300 g (11 oz) flaked Arbroath Smokie
  meat – about 3 Smokies
4 eggs, chilled
a splash of wine vinegar
salt and freshly ground black pepper
fresh watercress, to garnish
  (optional)

FOR THE SAUCE

2 large free-range organic egg yolks
salt and freshly ground black pepper
2 teaspoons lemon juice
2 teaspoons tarragon wine vinegar
100 g (3½ oz) butter
1 tablespoon freshly chopped
  tarragon (optional)

1. Shred the fresh sprouts in a food processor with the slicing disk, or by hand. Bring a pan of lightly salted water to the boil, add the sprouts and blanch for 1 minute. Drain well in a colander then refresh in cold water. If using cooked sprouts, chop them roughly.

2. Meanwhile, melt the butter in a pan, add the onion and bacon, cover and sweat gently for about 10 minutes, or until the onions are soft but not coloured and the bacon cooked. Tip into a bowl and mix with the mashed potato (if using leftover roast potatoes, cut them up roughly and squish them a bit with a potato masher) and sprouts. Season.

3. Shape into four potato cakes and fry these in foaming butter for about 7 minutes (in total), or until hot and golden brown on both sides. Keep warm.

4. To poach the eggs, bring a large pan of water to the boil and add a splash of wine vinegar. Crack each egg into a cup, stir the water into a whirlpool then slip an egg into the centre. Allow to spin for a few seconds then simmer gently for about 3 minutes. Remove with a slotted spoon and put into a bowl of warm water (this is to keep them warm if not using immediately). Repeat with the remaining eggs.

5. To serve, place the bubble and squeak cakes on a plate, set the flaked Arbroath Smokie on top then carefully place the drained poached eggs on top of the fish to form a stack. Serve with hollandaise (optional) and a handful of peppery watercress.

Easy hollandaise sauce

This recipe takes all the fear out of making hollandaise – just make sure that you get the butter very hot indeed before you pour it onto the eggs. Perfect with almost anything fishy.

1. Put the egg yolks, and a pinch of salt and freshly ground black pepper, into a food processor.

2. Put the freshly squeezed lemon juice and tarragon wine vinegar into a small pan and heat until it boils, then remove from the heat and with the processor running, immediately pour the hot liquid onto the eggs.

3. Melt the butter until it is foaming. Again, with the machine running, pour the boiling hot butter onto the eggs in a steady stream. The butter will thicken the egg yolks like a warm mayonnaise. Add the chopped fresh tarragon (optional). If you like, thin the hollandaise down by beating in a little warm water. Use immediately as this doesn't hang about.

smoked chicken with moroccan couscous

I was blown away by Moroccan food when Robert and I went to Marrakech for our 25th wedding anniversary. The spiced sweetness of the tastes and the heady souk air was so exotic. When we got home I was determined to create a dish to remind me of our magical holiday.

SERVES 4

55 g (2 oz) butter
6 spring onions, sliced
2 celery sticks, diced or sliced
a large pinch of ground cinnamon
1 chicken stock cube
55 g (2 oz) chopped apricots
55 g (2 oz) raisins
300 g (10 oz) couscous
55 g (2 oz) whole almonds, toasted
1 whole smoked chicken, flaked into large pieces

TO SERVE
chopped fresh coriander
3 tablespoons olive oil
1 teaspoon sweet or smoked paprika
¼ teaspoon cumin

1. Gently sauté the sliced celery and spring onions in the butter. Stir in the crumbled chicken stock cube, cinnamon, chopped apricots, raisins and couscous. Mix well. Pour in about 400 ml (²/₃ pint) boiling water (or enough to cover), cover with cling-film and leave to stand and swell for 10 minutes.

2. Meanwhile toast and roughly chop the almonds and warm the chicken.

3. When the couscous is ready, fluff it up with a fork and transfer to a large shallow dish. Pile the chicken on top and scatter with the almonds.

4. To serve, heat the olive oil in a small pan, then stir in the paprika and cumin. Drizzle over the dish and sprinkle with a little extra cinnamon and chopped corian-der. Serve with roasted red peppers and butternut squash.

Christmas smoked salmon roulade

A really eye-catching centrepiece for any celebration. Make sure you make extra as I promise everyone will want to cut themselves second helpings no matter how full they claim to be.

SERVES 4–6 AS A STARTER

FOR THE ROULADE
55 g (2 oz) butter
3 level tablespoons plain flour
300 ml (½ pint) milk
1 egg, separated
200 g (7 oz) smoked salmon, finely chopped
2 teaspoons lemon juice
3 tablespoons finely chopped fresh parsley

FOR THE FILLING
200 ml (7 fl oz) crème fraîche
200 g (7 oz) thinly sliced smoked salmon
¼ cucumber, very thinly sliced
salt and freshly ground black pepper

1. Preheat the oven to Fan 180°C/200°C/400°F/Gas Mark 6.

2. Grease and line a 20 x 30 cm (8 x 12 inch) Swiss roll tin with non-stick baking parchment.

3. Melt the butter in a saucepan and add the flour, cook for 1 minute then whisk in the milk, bring to the boil, stirring, and simmer for 5 minutes until thick. Cool until warm, then beat in egg yolk, smoked salmon, lemon juice and parsley. Taste and season. In a separate bowl, whisk the egg white until holding soft peaks then carefully fold into the salmon mixture using a large metal spoon.

4. Turn into the prepared tin and quickly level the mixture, spreading it out into the corners. Bake for 10–12 minutes until set and light golden brown.

5. When the roulade is cooked, invert onto a clean tea towel. Carefully peel away the baking parchment and loosely roll up from the short side like a Swiss roll. Cool.

6. When cold, carefully unroll the roulade, spread with the crème fraîche and lay the remaining smoked salmon on top and the sliced cucumber over this. Roll up again from the short side, using the tea towel to help you, then carefully transfer to a serving plate, seam-side down. Cover and chill until ready to serve. Serve cut into thick slices with extra crème fraîche and salad leaves.

Christmas canapés

I always like to do something special at Christmas and these deliciously different smoked salmon canapés make a great start to any party. Very easy to make: just open the champagne and have fun!

smoked salmon with ginger butter on oatcakes

100 g (3½ oz) butter, softened
20 g (¾ oz) fresh ginger, peeled and finely chopped
1 teaspoon grated lemon zest
2 teaspoons chopped fresh chives, plus extra to garnish
200 g (7 oz) sliced smoked salmon
About 20 small cocktail oatcakes
black pepper

1. To make the ginger butter, put the butter, ginger, lemon zest and chives in a small food processor and blend until smooth.

2. Using a spatula, spoon the butter mixture into a bowl.

3. To assemble, roll up small pieces of smoked salmon, spread a little ginger butter on an oatcake and top with the salmon.

4. Decorate with pieces of chive. Sprinkle with black pepper and serve.

125

royal fillet on rye with horseradish and tarragon cream, trout caviar

MAKES ABOUT 20

250g (9 oz) piece of smoked salmon royal fillet
200 ml (7 fl oz) crème fraîche
2 tablespoons creamed horseradish sauce
2 tablespoons chopped walnuts
2 teaspoons chopped fresh tarragon, plus 20 whole leaves to serve
300 g (10 oz) rye bread cut into 20 fingers
sea salt and freshly ground black pepper
50 g (1¾ oz) trout caviar

1. Cut the royal fillet vertically into 20 even slices.

2. Cut the rye bread into mini-rectangles to fit the fillet slices.

3. Mix the crème fraîche, horseradish, chopped walnuts and chopped tarragon together in a separate bowl. Season and spread generously onto the rye bread pieces.

4. Top each with a slice of royal fillet, a tarragon leaf and some trout caviar. Serve immediately.

smoked salmon and anchovy crisps

MAKES ABOUT 40

125 g (4 oz) plain flour
125 g (4 oz) butter, chilled and cubed
125 g (4 oz) grated Gruyère
1 teaspoon dried oregano
a squeeze of anchovy paste
125 g (4 oz) smoked salmon

1. Put the flour, butter, cheese, oregano and anchovy paste into a food processor and pulse until it becomes a dough and begins to stick together.

2. Tip out onto floured work surface and pat into a rectangle about 2 cm (¾ inch) thick. Wrap and chill for 30 minutes.

3. Preheat the oven to Fan 180°C/200°C/400°F/gas mark 6.

4. Cut thin slices from the dough and arrange on baking trays. Slice strips of smoked salmon and lay down the centre of each slice.

5. Bake for about 8–11 minutes until golden. Allow to firm up on the baking sheet before transferring to a wire rack to cool completely.

126

little smoked salmon, cream cheese and herb sandwiches

MAKES ABOUT 48

300 g (10 oz) cream cheese
2 garlic cloves, crushed
fresh lemon juice, to taste
100 g (3½ oz) mixed rocket leaves, watercress and dill
12 medium slices fresh sunflower seed rye or granary bread
sea salt
200 g (7 oz) smoked salmon

1. Lightly butter the bread slices to seal.

2. Put the cream cheese, garlic, lemon juice and herbs in a food processor and pulse for about 10 seconds. Spread the mixture evenly over all the bread slices and sprinkle with a pinch of salt.

3. Then top half of the spread slices with smoked salmon and cover with the rest of the slices (spread side down!) to make sandwiches.

4. Cut the crusts off if desired and neatly cut each sandwich into small triangles or squares.

5. Cover tightly with clingfilm until ready to serve, to prevent the bread from drying out and curling.

Inverawe Smokehouses: the company

Robert and Rosie Campbell-Preston established their family business, Inverawe Smokehouses, in 1974.

From the very start there was a natural delineation in the partnership. Robert took on production and operations, while Rosie concentrated on sales and marketing.

With very small beginnings – just one smoke box and a production shed at the end of the garden – the company has grown to become a household name. It is one of the leading independent smokeries in Britain, supplying top niche food halls nationwide, as well as running a highly efficient mail-order service.

Robert and Rosie have always maintained that the secret to their success has been their refusal to compromise their standards in any way. At Inverawe they still smoke the old way, using the hand-filled oak log fires and the old-style brick kiln. For this they have been recognised in the industry with numerous awards and have been named as one of Rick Stein's Food Heroes.

Inverawe Smokehouses
Taynuilt
Argyll
PA35 1HU
T: 08448 475 490
www.smokedsalmon.co.uk

By Appointment to
Her Majesty The Queen
Mail Order Smoked Foods & Hampers
Inverawe Smokehouses

GREAT
Taste
AWARDS

THE GUILD OF
FINE FOOD
RETAILERS
Established 1995

SOIL ASSOCIATION
ORGANIC STANDARD

index by product